The Human Resource
Challenge of
International Joint Ventures

The Human Resource Challenge of International Joint Ventures

DIANNE J. CYR

Foreword by Wayne Cascio

QUORUM BOOKS
Westport, Connecticut • London

Library of Congress Cataloging-in-Publication Data

Cyr, Dianne J.
    The human resource challenge of international joint ventures /
Dianne J. Cyr ; foreword by Wayne Cascio.
        p.   cm.
    Includes bibliographical references and index.
    ISBN 0–89930–919–4 (alk. paper)
        1. International business enterprises—Personnel management.
    2. Joint ventures—Personnel management.   I. Title.
    HF5549.5.E45C95   1995
    658.3—dc20   95–19465

British Library Cataloguing in Publication Data is available.

Library of Congress Catalog Card Number: 95–19465
ISBN: 0–89930–919–4

First published in 1995

Quorum Books, 88 Post Road West, Westport, CT 06881
An imprint of Greenwood Publishing Group, Inc.

Printed in the United States of America

The paper used in this book complies with the
Permanent Paper Standard issued by the National
Information Standards Organization (Z39.48–1984).

10   9   8   7   6   5   4   3   2   1

To my parents, Joan and Jim Manzer,
who have given me so much

Contents

IV. Special Issues

APPENDIXES

Foreword

While much has been written about the way that strategic human resource management (HRM) is *supposed* to operate, little is actually known about the way that it *does* operate in practice. Based primarily on in-depth research on four successful joint ventures in the United States and Canada, the book provides a rich storehouse of information about HRM operations in five key areas: communication, staffing, reward and recognition, training, and performance review.

In addition to the *description* of strategic human resource management, this investigation seeks to shed light on the more elusive questions regarding *how* and *why* the human resource management function operates as it does in the more specific context of international joint ventures. Given these objectives, the author has studied four ventures, each representing a marriage of partners from different national cultures. Three of the companies are 50/50 ownership ventures, while the fourth was a 60/40 split between the partners. All four ventures were in the manufacturing sector of the economy, although in different market niches. Moreover, all four practice Total Quality Management and high employee involvement as strategies for enhancing product quality and innovation. The companies aimed to be challenging and satisfying places in which employees could work.

Instead of choosing a sample of convenience, Dianne Cyr used a number of specific criteria to screen companies for inclusion in the study. The criteria were stringent, and certainly aggravated the problems normally associated with the conduct of field research. In fact, it took six months of intense effort to secure the companies for the investigation. I admire her fortitude and persistence in adhering to the criteria originally established. I know how hard she worked to secure the cooperation of the four joint ventures that she studied: Mayo Forest Products, OCG Microelectronic Materials, Siecor, and Diamond Star Motors.

In addition to interviews, Dianne also reviewed a wide variety of information about each joint venture and the strategic orientation of the parent companies. She consulted numerous documents about the joint venture operations, and, more specifically, about the human resource management function as it operated in each venture. While on site, she was involved in participant observation, attending meetings, and holding informal conversations with employees who came from multiple levels in the organization. In my view, this experience yields the kind of information that is almost impossible to obtain from strictly quantitative research, and yet it is extremely valuable to the development of theory.

To supplement information gained from the above sources, Dianne also administered several instruments to employees and managers. As a basis for doing so, she selected a systematic, stratified sample in each joint venture. These instruments were: the Minnesota Job Satisfaction Questionnaire, the Culture Inventory, and the Guide to Human Resource Management Practices. The integration of results from these data sources provided a mosaic of information about strategic human resource management, and a unified analysis of human resource management practices in each company.

This book should be required reading for anyone who is interested in this area. The insights on issues such as the management of the joint venture-parent relationship, the integration of human resource management and strategic planning, organizational learning, and corporate and national cultures represent true value-added knowledge. In addition, the work is a catalyst for a wide range of future research. In my view, Dianne Cyr has created a work of genuine value to the rest of the field.

Wayne Cascio

Preface

This book aims to capture the elusive people issues which influence the success dimension of international joint ventures. With the expansion of joint ventures in all corners of the world, the form and function of human resource management in globally-focused companies will receive increased attention. Managers and other employees will revise human resource operations in the context of transforming corporate strategies, and with consideration of cultural differences. Alternately, in companies where human resource management is of secondary concern, the chance to compete effectively by making use of people's strengths is dramatically diminished.

This book is written for both practitioners and academics. It is based on in-depth investigations of joint ventures in North America and Europe, and provides a summary of key issues for managers in these companies. It is surprising to find how similar the important human resource issues have been across all the joint ventures surveyed. Based on interviews with members at multiple levels in each company, I have aimed to synthesize the wisdom of the participants into some frameworks that build on previous research on this topic. This volume has the potential to provide practical and realistic insights for human resource management in international joint ventures, as well as spark avenues for further research.

I am especially grateful to the managers who allowed me entry into their organizations, and to all the participants in the investigation who gave so freely of their time and insights to this project. I would especially like to thank Jim Favier at OCG Microelectronic Materials, Sandy Fulton at Pacific Forest Products, Gary Garvey at Siecor, and Patrick Walter at Diamond Star, who were all instrumental in arranging my visits to companies in the North American sample.

I was particularly impressed by the rapid changes occurring in Poland, Hungary, and the Czech Republic during my visits to joint ventures in these regions during 1992 to 1993. The eagerness and dedication with which the local employees embraced transformational change was truly inspiring. Despite the obvious economic hardships in these countries, most people optimistically managed change, and were eager to work to maximal capacity to ensure a more stable future.

In addition, I would like to thank Peter Frost and Merle Ace at the University of British Columbia, who provided assistance in the course of the project. I appreciate generous funding from INSEAD International Business School in France for the Central/Eastern European phase of my research investigations.

Introduction

This joint venture is as unique as our people. Each individual with an astonishing variety of backgrounds and interests, and yet, each day we come together as one team—powerful, dedicated and satisfying to work with. Without people we would not have growth, and without growth, there would not be continued success.

Manager, Mayo Forest Products

The achievement of corporate success can only be accomplished by people. In an international marketplace where "borderless organizations" are quickly becoming the norm, employees have an increasingly important role in the cultivation of company achievements. The level of employee involvement in companies has expanded in general, and in internationally-oriented corporations, progressive managers recognize that only through the effective management of people can organizations survive.

This book is about how to enhance competitiveness in the most rapidly growing type of company—international joint ventures (JVs).[1] More specifically, its central theme is how strategic competence is stimulated in international joint ventures through human resource management (HRM).[2] Human resource management is broadly considered as it is enacted by HR managers and other staff in the venture. Strategy, culture, and innovation are analyzed in intersection with HRM policy and practice related to (1) how HRM reinforces the strategic firm objectives; (2) how diverse corporate cultures or national cultures are fused to result in synergistic outcomes; or (3) how HRM contributes to experimentation and innovation. As a critical component of organizational competence, HRM requires careful consideration related to the important role of people in complex organizations.

The insights expressed and descriptions offered in the following chapters are largely based on the experiences and wisdom of executives, managers, supervisors, production employees, and other staff in four progressive international joint ventures located in the United States and Canada. Their stories are vital and current, and contribute to new ways of understanding human resource management policy and practices in international joint ventures. In addition, this "window" from which to view HRM in joint ventures has resulted in practical HRM frameworks for other managers to consider. In each of the four joint ventures, HRM was a key to operational competitiveness related to quality, customer satisfaction, and production—and represents a trend in future organizations which is both a reality and a challenge.

HRM—A KEY TO SUCCESS IN JOINT VENTURES

Effective HRM practices are thought to be a significant contributing factor in the viability of a company. According to Likert (1967: 1),

Every aspect of a firm's activities is determined by the competence, motivation, and general effectiveness of its human organization. Of all the tasks of management, managing the human component is the central and most important task, because all else depends upon how well it is done.

In multinational corporations HRM has implications for corporate success (Evans, 1986; Laurent, 1986; Pieper, 1990; Schein, 1986; Schuler, 1989). Tichy (1988) notes the key to competitiveness in multinational companies is leadership and an innovative set of HRM practices which permit organizational flexibility and adaptability.

Despite a rapid increase in JV activity, previous information related to the development and implementation of HRM practice in international joint ventures is very limited. Although HRM is recognized as important and deserving of attention, the amount of time spent on HR issues in international ventures remains small. Frayne and Geringer (1989) note that "of the 100 to 5,000 hours typically involved in creating IJVs, only about 4% of the time has been spent resolving human resource issues."

The development of HRM policies and practices in international joint ventures presents special challenges for both managers and academics. HRM development and coordination is required not only within the venture, but *across* organizational boundaries between the venture and the parent firms as well. Intercompany relationships between the parents and the venture are an important, but overlooked phenomenon that requires greater focus. This sentiment is expressed by Ohmae (1990: 136), who observed,

> To my knowledge, however, not one scholar specializes in the study of *intercompany* [his emphasis] relationships. This is a serious omission, given the importance of joint ventures and alliances in today's global environment. We need to know much more than we do about what makes effective corporate relationships work. . . . We must recognize and accept the inescapable subtleties and difficulties of intercompany relationships. That is the essential starting point. Then we must focus not on contractual or equity-related issues, but on the quality of the people at the interface between organizations.

To meet the challenge for a better understanding of HRM in joint ventures, information is presented in this book related to human resource management, both in the venture and in the context of the venture-parent relationship. HRM operations are considered as they either enhance or limit the venture or parent strategic objectives. Considering how little information exists about HRM in joint ventures to date, this book aims to provide a comprehensive portrait of HRM as it operates in four manufacturing ventures, in order that both employees and the organization can prosper.

THE FOCUS OF THIS BOOK

Related to a need to better understand how HRM operates in JV firms, this book is focused on the important and strategic role that HRM has in international joint ventures. HRM is considered related to (1) management within the venture and (2) interorganizational management between the parents and the venture, or in some cases between the parent firms. Based primarily on a research investigation in four successful international joint ventures located in the United States and Canada, the evasive issues of *how* and *why* HRM operates as it does are explored in the areas of communication, staffing, reward and recognition, training, and performance review. Although a broad variety of topics related to HRM in joint ventures are analyzed, particular importance is given to the interrelationship of HRM with strategy and culture. Based on a new role for HRM in joint ventures, the following areas are highlighted:

1. *Joint Venture-Parent Relationship*—The relationship between the joint venture and parents is represented in both structural and strategic characteristics of how the joint venture is managed. Issues of importance include, for example, the assignment of management responsibility to one parent and how this affects how HRM operates; how trust is established between JV and parent representatives; and how integration of parent groups into the venture is accomplished.

2. *Integration of HR and Strategic Planning*—How HRM policy and practice sup-

ports or limits parent and joint venture strategic objectives is considered. For example, if there is a focus on quality and innovation in the joint venture, then HRM practices operate which reinforce this objective (e.g., selection of staff with broad skills who are able to work well in a team setting).

3. *Corporate Culture*—Attention is given to how norms and values are developed in the venture which support the strategic objectives of both the JV and parent firms. How parent norms and values are transmitted into the joint venture, versus the creation of a culture unique to the requirements of the joint venture, is discussed.

4. *National Culture*—The presence of different national cultures in the venture suggests consideration of cultural norms and values in the development of HR policy and practice. How HRM policy is created which is culturally appropriate and recognizes the needs of diverse groups is elaborated.

5. *Organizational Learning*—Reflected in both firm strategy and corporate culture, a capacity for learning at the organizational level is increasingly important to firm flexibility and survival. Learning is assessed at partner, administrative, and technological levels.

Based on information collected in the joint ventures in this project, HRM activities vary in each joint venture with reference to the preceding five considerations. For example, in joint ventures in which the parent cultures are diverse, the creation of culturally sensitive HR policy is potentially a central issue. In a start-up joint venture, the incorporation of parent groups into the venture and the establishment of a unified corporate culture may be a more pressing need.

AN OVERVIEW OF THE CHAPTERS

In this book a broad and complex role for HRM in international joint ventures is emphasized. Human resource policies and practices are described as they operate in four successful joint ventures. Each joint venture is ahead of expected targets on sales and financial indicators, and further, is generally considered by employees as a good place in which to work. To support company objectives, HRM practices are created to accommodate novel and challenging demands. HRM policy is ideally developed and implemented to reinforce the strategic firm objectives. Related to complexity in joint ventures which results from the combination of different parent cultures and goals, new forms of HRM are suggested that integrate people and values.

Many of the issues with which managers and other employees grapple are illuminated. HRM policy and practice are described as they operate within the ventures and provide information as to what is already being done in progressive joint ventures. In addition, new frameworks for understanding HRM in international joint ventures are suggested based on commonalties and comparisons across the four ventures that participated in this project. In Chapter 1, background is provided related to JV formation, benefits and difficulties of joint ventures, and special management issues including the JV board structure. The role of HRM in joint ventures is expanded in Chapter 2, including how multiple parent ownership and multiple national cultures affect HRM operations. In Chapter 3, the company strategic focus in each of the four ventures on Total Quality Management (TQM) (e.g., product quality and innovation, customer satisfaction, and cost efficiency) is discussed. How strategic objectives are accomplished through employee involvement (e.g., teamwork, "ownership" of work responsibilities, and problem-solving oriented toward continuous product and process involvement) is elaborated.

In Part II of the book the management of the relationship between the joint venture and the parent firms is outlined. More specifically, in Chapter 4, parent goals related to HRM operations are considered depending on whether the joint venture is "specialized" and the parents have relatively separate roles, or "value-added" and the parents contribute complementary expertise to the joint venture. Whether management of the joint venture is shared or more dominated by one partner also has implications for HRM and how it operates. Partner compatibility and the alignment of partner strategic intents is also considered. In Chapter 5, the assignment of management responsibility in the joint venture to one parent is discussed, and the influence of the managing parent company on HRM is explored. The role of venture managers in the creation of a separate identity for the joint venture, as opposed to adopting values and practices for the joint venture that mirror those in the parent firms, is considered.

Part III of the book is an in-depth analysis of HRM integrated with the strategic planning of the ventures. In Chapters 6 and 7, a new role for HRM is suggested that goes beyond the development of HRM techniques (e.g., the determination of routine reward entitlements or the calculation of recruitment requirements), to focus instead on the implementation of processes (e.g., the integration of diverse employee groups into the venture; how to deal with changing roles for managers and other employees). The determinants as to whether HRM is enabled to function in this role are outlined. In Chapter 8 the type and quality of communication systems which operate in the ventures, and between the venture and the parents, are analyzed. Constraints to information exchange, how communication systems operate across diverse cultural groups, and how technical information is shared between the venture and the parents are considered in the context of international joint ventures. Staffing is the topic of Chapter 9. How JV employees are screened and recruited, the exemplary level of personal and technical skills required, and the role of permanent and temporary transfers between the venture and the parent firms related to administrative and technological learning are outlined. In Chapter 10, a strong emphasis on training in all four ventures is discussed, along with the content of training programs and how training is provided. How monetary rewards are created in alignment with JV strategic objectives, or, alternately, inconsistencies between reward policy and practice which existed even in successful joint ventures is the topic of Chapter 11. Further, difficulties in the creation of nonmonetary recognition systems are discussed. In Chapter 12 performance reviews are considered related to their role in the ventures. In general, minimal attention is given to performance review by venture managers. National culture considerations are outlined with respect to how a special performance evaluation system was developed and implemented in an American-Japanese venture. Chapter 13 is an elaboration of some of the issues faced by JV managers and employees when parents represent diverse national cultures. In particular, how Japanese and American managers view culture (e.g., values, operating styles), and how HR policy is developed and implemented which is sensitive to the requirements of different groups in the venture are summarized.

Drawing on data from another research investigation in Poland, Hungary, and the Czech Republic, in Chapter 14 key issues facing HRM are considered in joint ventures formed between Western European partners and local partners. Of special interest is how HRM policy and practice can facilitate the transition from a planned to a market-oriented system in companies in Central/Eastern Europe. The role of the Western partner in contributing investment, technical, and managerial expertise is discussed. Finally, Chapter 15 offers a summary of the opportunities and challenges for HRM in global organizations of the future.

THE COMPANIES

The four international joint venture companies in which information for this project was collected are all competitive, strategic players in the global marketplace. In each case, the joint venture is successful by external standards of recognition for performance (e.g., customer awards), and is considered by employees as a positive place in which to work.

The joint ventures are all located in North America, and are formed between two international partners, each from a different national culture. The ventures share very similar corporate goals and objectives. Without exception, in all the joint ventures, employees strive to produce high-quality products in their respective market sectors. "Total quality" programs operate to accomplish this goal through (1) the reduction or elimination of defects, (2) continuous product improvement, and (3) the development of enhanced understanding of customer requirements. Employees are expected to actively contribute to this process through their involvement in quality management and product innovation. Depending on the reasons for the formation of the venture, the parents either have specialized roles or strive to combine their technological expertise in order to add value to the JV operation. Technology from the parent firms is transferred to the venture, depending on specific JV requirements.

The joint ventures are Mayo Forest Products, OCG Microelectronic Materials, Inc., Siecor, and Diamond Star Motors (DSM). An overview profile of the joint ventures in this research appears in Table 1. The joint ventures are balanced (2:2) related to age, number of employees, and whether or not the company is unionized.

Mayo Forest Products, established in 1980, is a small lumber manufacturing firm with 160 employees. It operates primarily as a subsidiary operation of Pacific Forest Products (60 percent owner), and is unionized. The other parent is Mitsubishi (40 percent) and provides Mayo Forest Products with access to the Japanese market. OCG Microelectronics, formed in January 1991, is a 50/50 partnership between American Olin and Swiss Ciba-Geigy, both multinational parent firms in the microelectronics industry. OCG is very decentralized, relatively small (196 employees), and non-unionized. Siecor was established in 1977 as a 50/50 equity venture between Corning and the German parent firm Siemens. Siecor specializes in fiber optics and maintains technological linkages with Siemens. This company is medium-sized (1,250 employees) and operates without a union. The final company to participate in this research is an automobile manufacturing joint venture which was formed in 1985 and began production in 1988. Diamond Star Motors is unionized, relatively large (approximately 3,000 employees), and the product of a union between Chrysler and Mitsubishi.

Mayo Forest Products

Mayo Forest Products is a Canadian-Japanese joint venture located in Canada. Mayo competes internationally in the high-quality lumber market. Logs entering the mill must be accurately cut to specified lengths and be free of defects in order to maximize lumber extraction and minimize waste. Eighty-five percent of the lumber manufactured at Mayo is sent to Japan, which represents approximately 4.5 percent of Japan's total North American lumber imports.

During construction of the mill in 1979, there was high participation from Mitsubishi in both the engineering and design phases of the project. When the mill began production in 1980 it was recognized in the industry as very progressive, and set a standard for quality requirements in the Japanese market. The plant came up to production quickly and maintained the same level for about seven years. During this time other competitors were outpacing the Mayo operation, productivity levels were not improving, and the plant technology was becoming outdated. There was no long-term plan, no formal quality control programs, and little information was shared with employees. Accidents in the mill were steadily increasing.

(continued)

TABLE 1
JOINT VENTURE PROFILES

	MAYO	OCG	SIECOR	DSM
Plant Start-up/ Reorganization	1980; reorg. 1988	1991 (January)	1977 reorg. 1988	1988
Ownership	60% Pacific FP 40% Mitsubishi	50% Olin Corp. 50% Ciba-Geigy	50% Siemens 50% Corning	50% Chrysler 50% Mitsubishi
Strategy Orientation	total quality management high employee involvement			
Management Contract	Pacific FP	Olin Corp.	Corning	Mitsubishi
Number of Employees	160	196	1250	3000
Union Status	unionized	non-union	non-union	unionized
Market Sector	lumber	photoresists/ polyimides	fiber optics	automobile
JV Type (Specialization or Value-Added)	specialization	value-added	value-added	specialization
Technology Transfer	none	both parents	both parents	Japanese

To counter this downward trend, in 1988 a Vice-President in Pacific Forest Products hired a new General Manager for the mill to transform the operation. To assist in the development and implementation of this change, an outside consultant worked with the General Manager and other staff members at Mayo Forest Products. As a result, a "High Performance Management System" was implemented to emphasize setting and meeting high quality standards; employee education and involvement; and statistical monitoring and communication of performance results to all levels of the organization. Part of the reorganization plan involved refocusing the goals and roles of each of the JV parents. The Japanese parent was to concentrate solely on marketing to Japan and would provide product-related information. Maintaining a supply of logs to the mill and management responsibility for the operation was given to the Canadian parent.

OCG Microelectronic Materials, Inc.

OCG is an innovative supplier of photoresist and polyimide products and services to semiconductor customers on a worldwide basis. Photoresists are specialty chemicals consisting of polymers and sensitizers which are used to create the pattern of electronic circuitry on silicon wafers used in semiconductor manufacturing. Polyimides are high-performance polymers used in fabrication and packaging of advanced semiconductor devices, including multichip modules. To maintain a solid market position as a supplier to fast-moving semiconductor companies, OCG products must meet specific customer requirements and be of an impeccable quality and standard. OCG employees are committed to meeting customer demands for product quality, on-time delivery, packaging, technical problem-solving, and innovation. Product marketing is to Europe, North America, and the Pacific Rim.

OCG is a "value-added" joint venture which synergistically combines the unique technological capabilities of Corning and Ciba-Geigy. OCG operates with a TQM philosophy and focuses on high employee involvement to meet the company's entrepreneurial goals of innovation and customer satisfaction. Related to corporate strategic objectives, early successes were achieved in the new venture. In 1991, after approximately six months of operation, OCG was already number three in the microelectronics industry. The JV president strives for continuing excellence and stated the dedication to quality at OCG "will drive our quest to become the premier worldwide supplier of advanced microelectronic materials. Indeed, it is my intention that by 1995, OCG will be the company which other specialty chemical suppliers use as a benchmark for excellence."

OCG is both complex and decentralized. Headquarters offices are in the United States. Product manufacturing is in the United States with an additional manufacturing facility planned for Europe. Research and Development is undertaken in the United States and Switzerland, and is coordinated on a global basis. To maintain close customer relations, customer support and technical service centres are located in the United States, Belgium, and Japan. According to staff in the venture, OCG is currently the only photoresist supplier with research and development, manufacturing, technical customer support, and

(*continued*)

marketing capabilities in all three major electronics markets of the world (i.e., Europe, North America, and the Pacific Rim). This unique feature makes OCG an example of a "triad alliance."

Siecor

Siecor is currently the world's largest independent manufacturer of fiber optic cable; the company also makes supporting components such as cable connectors and electro-optic products. These commodities are used in increasing quantities in telephone networks and cable television systems, as well as in other areas of the telecommunications industry. Siecor internationally markets fiber optic cable and strives to be a total quality supplier which consistently meets customers' requirements on time and without defects or errors. The corporate office for the company is located in a small town in the eastern United States. Manufacturing is undertaken at four plants. Two plants are within several kilometers of the corporate office, and primarily manufacture fiber optic cable. The other plants make elevator control cables and related support equipment which is sold to the telecommunications industry. Siecor also has a distribution center and regional sales offices.

The parent companies, Corning and Siemens, contribute complementary expertise to the joint venture. Siemens is an international manufacturer of telecommunications equipment, electrical and electronic components, and subsystems. It provides technical expertise in cable development to Siecor, and has designed much of the equipment used by the joint venture in the cable manufacturing process. Technical staff are transferred from Germany to Siecor on a temporary basis to assist in the implementation phase of new equipment or technology. Corning is a world leader in the development of high-grade optical fibers, and is the primary supplier of optical fibers to the joint venture.

Although originally established in 1977, in the period around 1991 the joint venture underwent a strategic reorientation to focus more on quality and to encourage employee involvement. A redesign program in both plants was aimed at introducing team-based manufacturing to the operation. In one of the plants, an experimental group of employees was organized into work cells and minifactories which are given responsibility for the completion of units of work from start to finish.

Diamond Star Motors (DSM)

Located in the United States, DSM is the product of the Chrysler-Mitsubishi union.[3] The American parent is one of the "Big Three" automobile manufacturers in the United States; the Japanese partner is part of a highly integrated and industrialized network of companies located in both Japan and around the world. The decision to create a joint venture in the auto manufacturing industry was the result of approximately 20 years of cooperative relationships between the two parent firms. Diamond Star manufactures a line of sporty coupes and sedans which are marketed in Japan and in the United States. The manufacturing site includes a two million-square-foot building and a one-and-a-half-mile

(continued)

oval test track. The manufacturing and assembly facility has a stamping shop, a plastics molding operation, a body shop, a paint shop, and a trim and final assembly area. Diamond Star is one of the most technically advanced auto assembly plants in the world, with more than 470 robots in operation. At full production, Diamond Star has the capacity to produce 240,000 vehicles annually, or 63 cars per hour.

Although the joint venture was announced in 1985, it took two years to finish the construction of the plant. The plant site was chosen due to its close proximity to various transportation systems, and because the Japanese parent was offered an attractive state grant to build in the area. From the initial JV formation in 1985, each parent firm had a planning task force in operation. One task force was located in the United States, the other in Japan. Groundbreaking for the plant began in 1986, and the first cars rolled off the assembly line in 1988, two months ahead of the estimated schedule. Success came early to Diamond Star. In 1989, DSM was named one of the Top Ten Outstanding Engineering Achievements for 1988 by the National Society of Professional Engineers. Diamond Star models rank as some of the best cars in several automobile magazines.

SOURCES OF INFORMATION

Both formal, institutionalized HR practices and informal operating systems were considered in each joint venture. Information about HRM in each venture was collected primarily through interviews and questionnaires. Approximately 20 interviews were conducted at multiple levels in each company. In general, all senior managers were interviewed, as well as HRM managers and staff, select mid-level managers, a union representative (if applicable), and production workers. A broad sampling of employees allowed a "non-management" as well as a management view to be expressed. In some cases, employee perceptions of how HR policy and practice actually operated were at variance with stated company objectives. For example, production workers mentioned that supervisors selectively withheld information from employees despite a mandate encouraging open communication. Although training and rewards for performance are important in each joint venture, heavy production schedules interfered with training programs. Further, production employees are seldom rewarded specifically for performance or skills related to the accomplishment of strategic objectives.

The interview format was consistent for all participants and the sessions were tape-recorded. In addition, two different questionnaires were distributed to a stratified random sample of employees in each joint venture to measure job satisfaction and employee perceptions of the JV corporate culture. To gather information about the joint venture more generally, and HRM policy and practice more specifically, a wide variety of documents were reviewed (e.g., company newsletters, employee handbooks, company brochures or manuals, JV annual reports, policy statements, HR forms, newspaper articles on the joint venture, and union agreements). During full-time attendance on the JV site, I attended a variety of meetings, toured manufacturing operations, and had informal conversations with employees at multiple levels in the organization.[4]

NOTES

1. The term "joint venture" refers to a legally independent organization which is the product of the partnership of two corporations (the parent firms), each of which participates in the decision-making activities of the jointly-owned company. In an international joint venture (IJV), at least one parent firm has its headquarters outside the country where the joint venture is located.

2. HRM in international joint ventures includes (1) communication through informal and formal mechanisms for information exchange in the joint venture and between the joint venture and parents; (2) staffing through temporary or permanent assignment of parent personnel to the joint venture and new hires; (3) monetary reward and non-monetary recognition for employee achievements; (4) training in technical and interpersonal areas; and (5) performance review to determine past and future employee accomplishments. Refer to Appendix 1 at the end of this book for a further description of HRM activities.

3. Shortly after data collection for this project, Mitsubishi bought out Chrysler to become the sole owner of the venture.

4. Refer to Appendix 2 at the end of this book for a more detailed explanation of the methodology used in this investigation, including interview questions and sample questionnaires.

PART I

Competing for Success

CHAPTER 1

The Joint Venture Phenomenon

> Globalization is the integration of business activities across geographical and organizational boundaries. It is the freedom to conceive, design, buy, produce, distribute, and sell products and services in a manner which offers maximum benefit to the firm without regard to the consequences for individual geographic locations or organizational units. There is no presumption that certain activities must be located in certain places or that existing organizational boundaries are inviolable. . . . The global firm is not constrained by national boundaries as it searches for ideas, talent, capital, and other resources required for its success.
>
> Barnett (1990: 7–8)

To compete in an international business environment, firms are forming joint ventures as a mechanism for the enhancement of global competitiveness. In recent years, an explosion of IJV activity signifies this form of alliance as a popular vehicle for augmenting strategic capability.[1] International joint ventures are formed for a variety of reasons. International companies create venture partnerships to gain foreign market access, for the acquisition of new technology, to fund capital requirements beyond the capability of a single firm, or in order to share risks. Joint ventures are also a vehicle through which companies can gain broader scale sourcing of materials required for their operations. The possibility exists for both the joint venture and parent firms to learn new skills from one another, and to share technology or information as a result of the venture. Many of these elements are essential ingredients for companies that aim to compete in an international arena—where competition is fierce, and where requirements for quality, innovation, and meeting customer requirements are critical.

Although there are clearly potential economic and technological benefits that result from firms venturing together, the failure rate of joint ventures is high. For example, in a study of 880 joint ventures and co-operative alliances, only 45 percent of the companies were judged successful by all sponsors (Collins and Doorley, 1991). Some factors that lead to JV failure include: significantly different goals of parent firms; perceptions of unequal costs and benefits; and conflicts over decision-making, managerial processes, and corporate values (Dymsza, 1988; Killing, 1983). Misunderstanding is most likely when international joint ventures span diverse national cultures, and when attitudinal and value differences exist between different groups in the venture (Baird, Lyles, and Wharton, 1989). Problems often arise when executives in the parent companies attempt to impose their standards and policies for operation on the joint venture firm.

THE FORM AND FUNCTIONING OF JOINT VENTURES

International joint ventures represent a unique form of the globally-oriented corporation, with the greatest incidence of collaborative agreements between two partners (Hergert and Morris, 1988). The management of joint ventures is a complex process. If parent firms decide that a joint venture is required to accomplish desired strategic goals, then the partners must be prepared to deal with difficult issues related to joint ownership and joint decision-making in the venture. Collins and Doorley (1991) observe that in successful joint ventures, much advance planning is required, and the venture is likely to be championed by senior executives in the parent firms.

The venture plan will ideally consider market options, business strategy, resource requirements, and funding—all related to partner compatibility. Collins and Doorley elaborate that company style and corporate culture should be a "major consideration" as to whether two parent firms are able to effectively come together in a joint venture operation. Different goals, perceptions, and values of parent firms may result in corporate disharmony, and frequently to the failure of the venture (Dymsza, 1988; Killing, 1983). For example, do prospective JV partners have similar operating styles related to decision-making and HR management? Is there partner compatibility related to the level of employee participation desired in the joint venture? To avoid misunderstanding between the partners, these issues might be addressed in early JV negotiations, before the actual start-up of the venture.

In addition to planning for the venture, Collins and Doorley (1991) suggest other criteria which will enhance the success of various forms of strategic alliances. These "golden rules" of partnership success include:

- a balance of trust and self-interest
- anticipation of conflicts
- clear definition of strategic leadership
- flexibility
- acceptance of cultural differences at the level of both the national culture and the corporate culture
- orchestration of technology transfer
- learning from the partner's strengths

Taken together, the preceding points offer some guidelines for how the relationship between joint venture partners might best be managed.

BALANCING STAKEHOLDER INTERESTS

In early venture negotiations, the parents need to decide who has management responsibility for the venture, in which specific areas, and how key positions in the venture are to be staffed. In addition, the level of autonomy and decision-making responsibility allocated to JV managers (as opposed to parent managers) must be decided. For the venture to achieve maximal results, members of both the joint venture and parent organizations will work toward the success of the venture. Lorange and Roos (1992; 1991) point out that there are two political considerations in strategic alliances. These are:

- *Stakeholder Blessing*—Are both internal (e.g., JV) and external (e.g., parent) interest groups convinced that the venture is desirable?
- *Internal Support*—Are a broad range of employees in the venture convinced that the venture is viable? Are they committed and able to further the JV goals?

Related to internal support, if managers and other groups in the venture perceive a threat to their careers or personal goals, then enthusiastic, positive contributions to the venture are likely to be curtailed.

The extent to which HRM or other strategic management practices are adopted from one parent influences the corporate culture and dominant values present in the venture. For example, Frayne and Geringer (1989) propose that training content, the form of performance appraisal, and the type of compensation and reward will affect the JV corporate identity. If one parent has management responsibility for the joint venture, then theoretically that parent is more likely to infuse the venture with its practices, strategic objectives, and operating style.

The development of a corporate identity in the venture is likely to occur under some of the same conditions which operate in wholly owned companies. Various authors (Joiner, 1987; Kanter, 1989; Morgan, 1988; Schein, 1986; Walton and Lawrence, 1985) suggest that an integrated corporate identity is most likely when:

- there is strong, unified leadership;
- there is a vision and mission statement for the company which is meaningful to employees and continually reinforced;
- communication is open at all levels in the organization;
- employees are actively involved; and
- HRM practices reinforce company values.

In joint ventures, evidence of these characteristics may contribute to the development of a unified JV corporate culture which is independent from that of the parent firms.

THE JV BOARD STRUCTURE

Most joint ventures have a dual-board structure which includes (1) a formal Board of Directors that is usually comprised of senior representatives of both parent firms; and (2) an advisory committee that is often the operating group for the venture. Generally, the Board of Directors is concerned with the ongoing success of the venture, as well as the protection of parent interests. The Board typically approves the annual operating plan, reviews budgets, and approves major capital expenditures. According to Collins and Doorley (1991), in a 50/50 joint venture the Board would usually have equal representation from each of the parents. Members of the Board are chosen to "reflect the main contributions of each parent." The General Manager of the venture will often sit on the Board, but may not always have full voting rights. At OCG, Siecor, and Diamond Star there is equal representation from the two parents on the JV Board; at Mayo Forest Products the Board is comprised of three members from the Japanese parent and four members from the Canadian parent firm. At Mayo, this unequal distribution reflects the larger degree of management and operations involvement by the Canadians.

To elaborate, at Diamond Star the Board of Directors consists of eight members, four from each parent company. The Chairman of the Board; the Executive Vice-President of Finance; the Executive Vice-President and Senior Manufacturing Advisor; and the Vice-President and General Manager for Procurement and Supply are employees of Chrysler. Alternately, the President and Chief Executive Officer; the Executive Vice-President of Manufacturing, Procurement and Supply and Quality Control; the Executive Vice-President, Human Resources and Administration; and the Vice-President, Assistant to the President are employees of Mitsubishi. All executive officers are actively involved in the management of Diamond Star.

According to one of the Japanese Vice-Presidents, the Board of Directors of Diamond Star operates on a "unanimous consensus basis" in which there is "agreement through discussion." The consensus management style was established early on in these meetings by the JV President. The Japanese vice-president remarks,

There is not a single case where we couldn't come to agreement. Very fortunate. Maybe because except one person out of the four Chrysler guys . . . Chrysler has been associated with Mitsubishi for about 20 years. So there is some inclination to understand the Japanese business, or the Mitsubishi business in relation to Chrysler. So it's not the combination of two strange parties, and this might have helped consensus.

If serious differences of opinion between the two parent firms arise, they are not handled through a process of third party arbitration, common in large North American corporations. Instead, issues are settled by the President of Diamond Star who represents Mitsubishi, and the Chairman of Board representing Chrysler.

The management group responsible for OCG operations consists of a President, Technical Director, Financial Director, and two Business Directors for North America and Europe. The President of the joint venture reports to a six-person Board of Directors, with a Board Chairman who rotates between the parent companies. There are four board meetings a year that members agree operate effectively. To some extent this may be a product of tolerance and interpersonal "chemistry." As the President of OCG remarks, "the parents in a joint venture are generally much more tolerant of their joint ventures than they are of their own individual businesses because they don't want to look to their partner as if they're not being reasonable." The main issue of contention so far—the location of the European manufacturing facility—was settled in a manner amenable to both partners. Several of the senior managers alluded that the joint venture is working well because the two most senior board members, each representing a parent company, get along well on a personal level. There is also good communication between these senior executives and the rest of the management group.

THE ROLE OF THE JV ADVISORY COMMITTEE

The JV advisory committee is comprised of senior managers in the venture, and is active in the day-to-day operation of the company. The advisory committee informs the Board of Directors of key issues for consideration when Board approval is required. At OCG, for example, the advisory board consists of one senior manager from each parent (who are both on the Board of Directors), and three additional members from each parent firm. Of the eight-person advisory board, six of the members are able to vote and there are two non-voting members. The advisory board meets every four to six weeks. At Diamond Star, the operating committee consists of the JV President plus four Executive Vice-Presidents, two from each of the parent companies. The President of Diamond Star is an employee of Mitsubishi, so in total the Japanese parent has three votes to Chrysler's two. One of the Japanese Vice-Presidents states that the purpose of this split vote is to avoid "deadlocks."

At Mayo Forest Products, the advisory committee meets quarterly (or more frequently), and alternates between locations in Japan and Canada. The advisory committee has a central role in how the mill is managed. A senior manager in the Canadian parent company states,

If there are other issues that need to be addressed at the senior, and when I say the senior level, the Board of Directors level, we would look to the advisory committee as the vehicle to develop the direction or the consensus of what steps we're going to take. That might be as complex as negotiating the next agreements that will prevail for the next ten years in how the ownership structure is going to take, or what sales agreements are going to be, or log supply agreements or you know generally the parameters in which the two companies own the operation. So any one of those issues that might come up would be dealt with either at the advisory committee level or in a subcommittee, if you will, of those individuals. So those individuals at the advisory committee level play a very integral role in the management of the operation and dealing with any of the issues between the two owners. And that might not be so evident when you're sitting at the mill.

LESSONS LEARNED

As complex organizational entities, joint ventures deserve special attention in the earliest stages of formation concerning how the joint venture is structured and managed. In many cases, managers overlook the subtleties inherent in ventures that can lead to failure. In order to maximize opportunities for success, managers should consider:

1. the degree to which there is consistency and commonality in the goals of parent firms, and whether parent expectations for the future of the joint venture are in alignment;
2. whether the corporate cultures of the parent companies are compatible;
3. the level of advance planning required to adequately determine issues such as how decision-making will be shared, appropriate levels of involvement by each parent, and how key positions will be staffed;

4. whether there is "stakeholder blessing" from all key parties with financial or moral investments in the joint venture;

5. the degree to which responsibility for the management of the venture is shared (or should be shared) between JV managers and managers in the parent firms; and

6. how best to structure the joint venture board and advisory committees in order that both parents as well as key players within the venture can provide balanced and constructive input into strategic and operational initiatives required for the venture.

NOTE

1. Refer to Collins and Doorley (1991), Harrigan (1985), Killing (1983), and Shenkar and Zeira (1987) for an elaboration of joint ventures. Lewis (1990) offers a comprehensive text which includes management issues in various forms of strategic alliances.

CHAPTER 2

HRM *in International Joint Venture Firms*

> HR, in many ways, sits in the middle of a company. It has a central position because HR deals with production, the union, the parents, and diverse cultures and as a result you're tap dancing on bonfires all the time. . . . Of all the myriad of problems you couldn't even imagine happening—they have happened.
>
> HR Manager, Diamond Star

Management issues in joint ventures are extremely complex, and encompass an ability by managers to create a cooperative relationship between the JV partners when multiple national cultures, corporate cultures, and partner strategies are combined. More specifically in the realm of HRM, Cascio and Serapio (1991) found trust building, job design that enhances learning, well-defined recruitment and staffing policies, and training programs and fair compensation policies to be salient issues in joint ventures. Although many of these issues are also relevant in wholly-owned companies, complexity is added to how HRM operates when multiple parent firms are involved. For this reason, early planning in joint ventures is especially important in order that differences in cultural and management styles between the parents and the venture are considered (Datta and Rasheed, 1989).

Further, in globally focused companies, there exist special requirements for learning, innovation, and transformation. As Parkhe (1991) describes, in strategic alliances an ability to learn is crucial to the attainment of organizational successes. HRM systems can either support or curtail an environment for learning (Pucik, 1988). Learning occurs as HRM policies are adjusted to meet new demands in the joint venture based on multiple partner needs, or the presence of diverse national culture norms or values.

As organizations change, so does the configuration of HRM. The "new version" of HRM has more fluid boundaries—and HRM managers and others in the organization join hands in accomplishing the company vision and strategy. To varying degrees, the HR function is able to realize its potential as a strategic player in the organization—a role that is continually expanding and contracting to include strategist, caregiver, forger of innovative policy, and integrator of culture and values.

HRM ISSUES IN JOINT VENTURES

Shenkar and Zeira (1987: 549) observe that in "the vast majority of the literature on JVs, issues about human resources are sporadic and limited." Some topics that are either little understood or problematic include staffing, promotion, loyalty of employees to the joint venture, decision-making, communication, and compensation. In addition, the authors note that research to date has ignored many fundamental HRM issues in joint ventures such as career development, termination of service, demotion, absenteeism, employee attitudes, control patterns, job design, training, and job rotation. Further, two structural characteristics of joint ventures that significantly affect HRM are not typically considered. They are:

- *Multiple Ownership*—Parent firms might differ related to: private or state-owned; size; reputation or competitive advantage; industry focus; whether or not they are unionized; human resource orientation; objectives for joining the venture; and the extent to which one parent tries to dominate the joint venture.

- *Multiple National Affiliation*—The joint venture is a setting for individuals who often differ in national origin, cultural values, and social norms.

To address some of the above concerns, Pucik (1988) examined the causes of HRM-related problems in 23 joint ventures established between American or European manufacturing firms and Japanese partners located in Japan. Pucik found low performance in the ventures was related to an inability on the part of the Western partner to manage the cooperative relationship related to cultural and strategic difference. More specifically, difficulties in the management of the joint venture were related to:

- *Staffing*—Frequent changes among Japanese managers resulted in inconsistent communication links with the Western partner; overreliance on the Japanese partner to obtain suitable recruits reduced control over staffing by the Western partner.

- *Training*—Utilization of external training programs failed to provide socialization of employees to the values and norms of the joint venture; the venture became a convenient training ground for the Japanese parent company.

- *Performance Appraisal*—Use of Western-style performance appraisal was inappropriate for Japanese staff related to cultural differences (i.e., preferences for group versus individual evaluation; level of explicit versus implicit feedback considered desirable).

- *Reward*—High wage costs resulted from a desire to attract employees from the Japanese parent firm; the Japanese perceived that Western expatriates were better compensated.

Other research further substantiates how the presence of managers from different national cultures adds to management complexity in international joint ventures. For example, Mendenhall and Black (1990) consider the subtleties of conflict resolution in Japanese-American ventures. The authors indicate (1) the Japanese do not view conflict and "harmony" on the same continuum (as the authors claim is the case with most Americans) and (2) the desire by Japanese to obtain harmony is specific to contextual conditions (i.e., whether "insiders" or "outsiders" to the group are present). These differences suggest implicit variations in conflict management styles between Japanese and Americans, which may or may not be apparent to the parties involved.

Ishida (1986) examined the transferability of Japanese values and practices to non-Japanese subsidiary operations and discovered that many of the problems were related to philosophical differences between the two groups. Ishida comments,

The difference in the concept of job leads to conflict between Japanese and non-Japanese working in the same organization. The non-Japanese cannot bear the vagueness of job boundaries and complain that the Japanese boss often trespasses on his own area of authority. The Japanese, on the other hand, criticize the non-Japanese workers for "doing only what they are told to do" and complain that they "lack initiative and flexibility."

Further, Tyebjee (1991) found that in venture partnerships between Japanese and Americans, differences exist related to strategic objectives and how information is controlled and managed. Peer task teams across the parent companies are viewed as one way to bridge strategic and cultural diversity. In addition, in earlier work by Peterson and Shimada (1978), communication difficulties between Japanese and American executives due to language differences were singled out as the most pressing problem in the ventures investigated.

In research in 37 joint ventures, Killing (1983) notes that managers of different nationalities have varying attitudes about fundamental assumptions regarding the importance of material wealth, the value of on-the-job performance and the desirability of change. According to Killing (1983: 57),

The greater the cultural gap between the parents' base countries, the greater the problem [in the international joint venture]. A fundamental hindrance to the creation of a core skill can simply be the difference in language. Many joint ventures formed in Japan in the 1960s between Japanese and North American firms failed in the early 1970s. Cultural differences were cited as a major problem in many of these.

The importance of understanding the cultural implications of international venturing is also underscored by Phillips (1989). In the investigation of a 50/50 American-Japanese joint venture, Phillips found that divergent management styles, inflated expectations, and disputes over quality and labor practices resulted in ongoing problems in the venture. Many of the differences in style and value orientations stemmed from national cultural heritage. Phillips comments (1989: 39),

[American] workers grumble about the daily calisthenics and the boring dedication ceremonies Japanese seem to love. And managers can't understand Japanese frugality. At one plant, the size of memo paper caused a 40-minute debate.

In an exploratory investigation conducted in the People's Republic of China, Teagarden and Von Glinow (1989) consider HRM in international joint ventures between Chinese and foreign firms. Teagarden and Von Glinow found that the cultural and social systems as they operate in China were a significant factor which affected JV effectiveness. More specifically, a Confucian influence, decision-making structures, the form and function of relationships, face-saving, and ideological assumptions influenced HRM. In other research, major attitudinal differences were found between American and Chinese managers in joint ventures regarding preferences for organizational structure, work orientation, and reward systems (Baird, Lyles, and Wharton, 1989).

In addition, Cascio and Serapio (1991) examined HRM in four international alliances. The authors considered issues related to the blending of national culture and management style, job design, staffing, training, performance appraisal, compensation and benefits, career issues, and labor-management relations. Cascio and Serapio summarize the lessons which are learned from their investigation:

• when national and corporate cultures are blended, the partners need to spend time building trust; understanding and accommodating each other's interests is important;

- job design can be enhanced when the partners are willing to learn from one another;
- recruitment and staffing policies should be well-defined in the early stages of the venture;
- orientation and training of employees should focus on preparing employees to deal with the social context of their jobs, as well as the development of technical skills;
- performance appraisals need clear objectives, liberal time frames in which to achieve results, and built-in flexibility related to changing market and environmental demands;
- compensation and benefits policies should be uniform to avoid employee feelings of inequity;
- career opportunities must be ensured for local managers; and
- in the early stages of the venture, the partners must agree on suitable terms for the labor-management agreement.

Considering these findings, time and precise planning are required to build a stable relationship between diverse partners in an alliance. HRM policy ideally is determined in the early stages of the venture, and is applied consistently. Datta and Rasheed (1989) conceptualize the importance in international joint ventures of planning with regard to the various conditions that affect HRM. Variables to consider in the planning process include the local labor market, differences in cultural and management styles between the parents, and parent objectives. Related to this last point, a degree of compatibility between parent objectives is important if venture partners are to work effectively together.

The partners may potentially learn new capabilities in an environment when there is an openness to new ideas and operating styles. Although learning and innovation are generally important in organizations, this capacity is critical in competitive corporations that operate on a global basis. One way in which learning is enhanced in joint ventures is through the development of flexible structures and relationships between the parents and the venture. Of increasing importance is the ability of JV managers to revise HRM and other systems in response to changing internal and external environments.

Pucik (1988: 77) advocates "the transformation of the HR system to support the process of organizational learning is the key strategic task facing the HR function in firms engaged in international cooperative ventures." According to Pucik, learning in alliances is more likely when there is:

- a high priority given to learning activities
- involvement by the HR function

- long-term planning
- a focus on obtaining and retaining high-quality staff
- training provided in cross-cultural competence
- a career structure which is conducive to learning
- reward and performance appraisal which focuses on long-term goals, learning activities, and global strategies
- incentive for the transfer of "know-how"
- an HR group having knowledge of the partner strategies

In addition, HR staff and other managers in the organization need to accept responsibility for the creation of conditions that result in learning. Learning is a process which requires integration. To enact this process, the HR department requires support from other managers and employees.

Various forms of strategic alliances have numerous stakeholders who are both internal and external to the alliance (Lorange and Roos, 1992; 1991). With respect to strategic and tactical changes in alliances such as joint ventures, support and approval of multiple interest groups (e.g., JV and parent employees) is advisable prior to transformations in organizational values or systems. To effectively implement learning and change, HR staff require knowledge of the concerns of various stakeholders (Kanter, 1983; Tsui, 1987), as well as the political skills necessary to manage change.

A DIFFUSED ROLE FOR HRM

The essence of what is HRM in today's organizations varies greatly. In most instances, the HRM role is fulfilled by the HR department working in conjunction with line staff in the company. HR managers in joint ventures find their function either confined or liberated by a wide range of internal and external organizational conditions which include:

- resource availability (staff, financial);
- level of support from stakeholders in the JV and parent firms;
- the degree to which HR managers are privy to strategic business information on the company;
- legislated work force policy or union stipulations;
- diversity and subsequently the ability to demonstrate the creation of culturally sensitive HR policy and practice;
- company size; and
- level of intended involvement by expatriate versus local managers.

Two of the joint ventures profiled in this book, Mayo Forest Products and Diamond Star, are between Japanese and North American partners. However, what HRM looks like in each company is very different. To a large extent, these differences result from the size of each venture and the intended involvement by each set of partners. A key factor influencing the role of HRM in the joint ventures is the number of expatriate managers on site, and hence the real requirement to create HR policy suitable to both the offshore partner and the largely American workforce.

To elaborate on the role for HR staff in each venture, at Mayo Forest Products (where there is minimal direct involvement by the Japanese in the mill and a relatively small number of employees), HR activities are managed largely by line staff, with some degree of coordination from a "Personnel/Safety Administrator." As indicated by the title, the role of the Personnel/Safety Administrator is largely focused on maintaining a safe work environment and the application of the union master agreement—with minimal emphasis on strategy-driven HRM. The Personnel Administrator observes, "they [the Canadian parent] believe that it's more of an administrative function where one person sort of acts as a monitor, resource person, even just in a clerical function making sure that everything is documented and filed." The performance management system that operates at the mill (including training, recognition, and employee involvement systems) was created by the General Manager, in conjunction with his management team and a group of consultants. Supervisors have primary responsibility for working with employees in human resource management areas. The Personnel Administrator at Mayo Forest Products states,

A lot of the personnel functions are handled by front line supervisors on a one-to-one basis. Pacific Forest Products believes that it is more of a supervisor's function to deal with his people than somebody that is removed sitting back in an office. I try to get out in the mill as much as I can, but I'm really not the front person. And so the supervisors basically do most of what you might call the human resource work—the one-to-one.

In this role, the personnel administrator has little direct input into policies and planning. However, the centrality of the function is indicated by the fact there is an adequate budget. The controller stated that if there were a need for funds in the personnel or safety areas, then the necessary funds would be allocated. Beyond a financial commitment, insufficient time allocated for HRM activities is an issue. The Personnel/Safety Administrator notes she would prefer to be more proactive than reactive in the development of HRM, but that this possibility is limited due to the large number of HRM responsibilities assigned to one person.

Alternately, at Diamond Star, where the Greenfield automobile plant required staffing a full complement of 3,000 workers and the creation of new HRM policy to meet the unique needs of the joint venture, the HR department (run jointly between Japanese and American managers) is important to the realization of strategic objectives. HR managers at Diamond Star indicate that a major challenge is to maintain a balance between various stakeholders in the plant (e.g., union-management and HRM-manufacturing). Early involvement and planning by HR staff have been critical to the successful launch of the venture.

To expand, HR planning began as soon as Diamond Star became a reality. The HR General Manager was hired in 1986, around the time construction began on the plant and 21 months prior to production start-up. The HR General Manager was the first "pure Diamond Star employee" to be hired into the operation, and he had not worked for either Chrysler or Mitsubishi previously. The Executive Vice-President for HR and the Assistant General Manager for HR are both from Mitsubishi, and also were assigned to the venture in the very early stages.

The task laid out for the newly-formed HR department was huge. Three thousand employees were to be hired, which meant processing about 200 to 250 people per month. Diamond Star received more than 80,000 employment applications, and although the selection of production associates was done through an assessment center operated by a consulting firm in the area, the HR department was responsible for input to the process. HR staff were actively involved in employee orientation, as well as in the recruitment of salaried employees and the development of benefit programs. Time was also spent preparing how to deal with the union, which management correctly anticipated would try to unionize Diamond Star. It was not until these issues had been dealt with that HR managers were able to turn their attention to policy formation.

THE IMPORTANCE OF EARLY DEVELOPMENT OF HRM POLICY

The volume of new policies required at Diamond Star was a source of frustration to many managers, and in some cases written policy was absent for a long time after operations began. Subsequently managers "made up their own [policies]." This created problems in the plant because managers did not know how to consistently handle HR-related situations such as insubordination, pay, and travel allotments. One production manager remarks that ideally policies, procedures, and rules of conduct should be determined in advance of when they will be required. To realize this goal, early planning and creation of HR policy is imperative—and underscores the related importance of early staffing of the HR group. A manager in the HR area voices these sentiments:

I think if there were two things I could say that were mistakes made, in terms of this particular joint venture, one of them was, and they kind of go hand in hand, one was not having a fully staffed human resources function on board before you brought anybody else in; and in conjunction with that was having your policies and procedures in place before you start hiring people. Because what was occurring in the absence of those policies, was, well, kind of what you felt like doing that particular day, or with that particular person. So I may have done something differently for you than what I did for the person I hired next month. And those have been some problems we're still living with to this date.

Part of the reason HR policies could not easily be set up early in the life of the joint venture was because of the pending unionization of the plant. The general manager of manufacturing notes that although certain policies should have been implemented earlier, with a new union there is "a gray area and if you create those policies early on then you're locking yourself into a situation where you don't have a lot of flexibility." In this case, when management waited to jointly work out some of the HR policies in conjunction with the union, a lag phase of approximately two years occurred between plant start-up and when the union was established at Diamond Star.

Managers in the HR department acknowledge they have numerous ongoing challenges. One HR manager mentions the difficulty in being proactive in a venture where they feel they are understaffed. He clarifies,

We'd like to take more of a leadership role, but we've been hampered in doing that from the standpoint that we don't have the number of people to do anything. Right now all we can do is react to things that happen. We can't be as proactive as what we should be. We can't be preparing better training programs, we can't be interacting better with the people because we have so many responsibilities and so few people to handle the responsibilities, that all we can really do is just jump from one project to the next. We don't have any time to do new projects.

This same manager remarks not having additional staff is a "major, major problem for human resources." Apparently the HR budget is one-half to two-thirds the size it would be for the same size operation in Japan, and much less than Japanese transplant companies in the United States.

CREATING A BALANCE

Some Diamond Star managers identify the major challenge for HR is in keeping a "balance" between groups in the plant that demonstrate different priorities. In particular, HR managers seek to maintain equilibrium between (1) union and management and (2) a human resources versus manufacturing focus. One manager in the HR group remarks,

It is important to keep the balance between the environment the Japanese have worked so hard to create on the floor with the associate people, and the environment the UAW [United Auto Workers] would like to create for their own reasons. How to keep the balance . . . and walk that fine line. To be able to walk that line, I think you need to know a great deal more than what we're learning, because you're liable to fall off and not know you have.

Related to the goals of both HR and manufacturing, a manager remarks the primary goal of manufacturing is to produce cars. HR is concerned mostly with "making sure people are treated as human beings," and sometimes practices which HR managers advocate for associates at Diamond Star may interfere with maximal production output. There have been instances, for example, when managers in manufacturing would like associates to work overtime, and may inform employees of this only a short time before they are due to leave work for the day. An HR manager mentions this is part of a difference in opinion between managers in manufacturing who want to get more time in on the line, and HR managers who feel it is their mandate to protect staff interests.

A STRATEGIC DIRECTION FOR HRM

In the quest to be strategic, the HRM group at Siecor more closely approximates this goal than do the other joint ventures. The HR function at Siecor is represented at several levels. At the highest level at the corporate office there is a Vice-President of Personnel who operates in an equivalent position to other vice-presidents in the company. Also located at corporate headquarters is a Personnel Manager responsible for the needs of administrative and managerial staff. In addition, the Manager of Employee Relations deals with issues pertaining to hourly and technical staff rather than with exempt, supervisory employees. Among other things, his role is to deal with legal issues, employment-related charges, and discrimination. There is a Personnel Department which reports to the Manager of Employee Relations. Employees in this department are primarily responsible for internal communications, worker's compensation and safety, recognition policies, company social functions, job evaluation, benefits, and compensation. Each plant has a Personnel Manager.

The HRM function is considered central in the strategic business planning process at Siecor. The Senior Vice-President of Personnel is a member of the executive planning group which meets with the JV President on a weekly basis to chart the course for the company. In referring to the HR function, one vice-president remarks the Personnel Vice-President is in a "position to see what's coming months ahead of anybody else . . . we people plan [in the executive sessions] once a week in a macro sense." He adds the Personnel Vice-President is "very active, very proactive in terms of causing the management to make decisions about people." Another executive who participates in these weekly management meetings remarks the first thing they do in the meeting is to look at "nosecounts" and the company standing on safety and other personnel issues. He mentions personnel is an "integral part of the business."

Related to the strategic role that HR has at Siecor, the Vice-President of Personnel comments,

One of the things we [in HR] are doing with our business plan is that we're driving more of the people part into that plan, which in previous years we didn't do very much of that. So in today's environment I think our role is to ensure that we have the kind of resources we need to meet the business conditions. . . . I must say that our people part of the company, the personnel piece of the company, is an integral part of the whole business planning process. . . . This gives us an opportunity to look at the business in terms of labor cost, in terms of all those kinds of costs that we have in terms of our wage and salary structures, our benefit plans.

Another HR manager sees an additional piece of the HRM role as "changing and/or emphasizing the company value system." This manager elaborates the important issues for Siecor are quality, employee involvement, team-based manufacturing and administration, diversity, safety, and compliance with environmental regulations. He sees the HR managers in the role of "initiator" of policies that meet the company goals. In the process of redesigning strategies to enhance employee involvement, members in the HR department can act as catalysts to expose line management to different modes of thinking related to work relationships.

At each plant, HR staff are given autonomy to create HR policy to meet specific plant requirements, while retaining the overarching strategic direction of Siecor. One plant manager observes,

At the plant level, we pretty much decide here what we're going to do. Now as things tend to become perhaps a little more of a departure from our history, we obviously talk to corporate personnel and have a lot of interaction there. For example, the trend has been to reduce the number of job classifications in the plant area and we've kept in touch obviously with the corporate group to keep us honest and make sure they don't have heartburn with some of the things we're proposing.

The HR managers at both plants are actively involved in the redesign of the plants to become environments more conducive to team participation. An HR manager in the plant comments that his role is "part of the plant leadership team, to develop the plant culture, to work to ensure the team activities give us the results we're looking for. To make sure that we don't violate any of the wage and hour . . . guidelines and laws. To help to develop the structure long-term that is going to make us successful."

In general, the joint venture has the opportunity to borrow HR policies from the parent companies, in this case primarily from Corning. As one HR manager explains,

The one thing we have been able to do at Siecor, which related to a company our size as compared to Corning or Siemens, is that we've been able to draw on the resources of both of those companies. We have been allowed to use systems of theirs if we chose to use them without them being driven down to us. So that's been a tremendous advantage and resource for us to be able to do that. Some things we have chosen to do the same—taking more from Corning than Siemens.

HR managers from Siecor participate in conferences in the human resource area organized from Corning. Through networking between the HR staff at both Siecor and Corning, HR policy information is exchanged informally. Although Siemens does not currently have HR conferences, the company is considering this possibility. If this were to occur, HR managers from Siecor would attend.

A continuing challenge for HRM is to perform at a high level of competency in order to avoid intervention from the parent companies. The senior HR manager mentions that only if HRM needs are adequately met in order to fulfil the business plan for Siecor will the joint venture be allowed to operate autonomously. This manager sees a second important challenge to the HR department as the avoidance of union intervention. Both parent companies are unionized, and occasionally the union has indicated an interest in the unionization of Siecor as well.

LESSONS LEARNED

The role for HRM in international joint ventures is both complex and diffused, and is interfaced with the special internal and external conditions that exist for companies in which interorganizational coordination is required. More specifically, for HR managers to attain maximal efficiency the following criteria deserve consideration:

1. planning for HR staffing and other needs will be completed in the earliest stages of the venture, and involve input from both parents;
2. ideally, the HR department will be fully staffed prior to hiring the majority of employees, and decisions must be made about staffing from the parents versus hiring of HR talent directly to the joint venture;
3. HR policies and procedure will largely be developed before staffing in the joint venture begins;
4. sufficient staff and other necessary resources will be allocated to the HR group;
5. the senior manager for HR will have an equivalent position to other senior operations managers;

6. the HR department will be provided with relevant strategic business information (e.g., related to JV and parent goals) in order to formulate HR plans and strategy to meet corporate objectives; and

7. HR managers (or other managers responsible for HR activities) will be given autonomy to make necessary policy changes as required.

CHAPTER 3

Strategic Profiles of Four Successful International Joint Ventures

We're trying to give opportunity for our employees to empower themselves, to do more, to be better employees, to take more responsibility, to internalize the quality process. By cross-training . . . it gives these employees the opportunity to learn more, to develop their skills more, and they really take more ownership for the whole process they're working on.

Manager, Siecor

In the context of world-class international organizations, the status quo has been discarded in favor of new forms of how work is done to achieve maximal results. Hierarchies are inevitably cast aside; static forms of organizations are insufficient; and increasingly, the skills of employees are used in flexible and fluid ways that lend continuous improvement to an organization's policies, methods, and structures.

In all the international joint ventures in this investigation, the corporate recipes for success are almost identical. In each company an emphasis prevails on Total Quality Management accomplished through high employee involvement. A key to success in each organization is management's commitment to creating a better organization in which employees can prosper. In turn, organizational relationships are rapidly transformed. Union-management interactions are changed, power is shifted from mid-level managers to the production floor, and production employees are asked to accept more responsibility—whether they want to or not.

JOINT VENTURE OBJECTIVES

There is much similarity in the strategic management goals and objectives that aim to facilitate the success of Mayo Forest Products, OCG, Siecor, and Diamond Star. Staff in all four companies strive to implement a Total Quality Management system that will enhance production creativity and innovation; consistently meet internal and external customer requirements on time, every time; and demonstrate cost efficiency. Employees are encouraged to be involved in decision-making in their work areas through systems which focus on teamwork, "ownership" of work responsibilities, and problem-solving oriented toward continuous product and process improvement.

In the determination of strategic initiatives, each of the joint ventures has an established model from which to draw insights and methods. At Mayo Forest Products, managers employed a consulting company to help with the company reorganization plan. OCG adopted the Total Quality Management system that operates at the American parent (Olin Corporation), and which was originally modeled after 3M (Minnesota Mining and Manufacturing Company). Further, OCG was deliberately structured to operate as a small and innovative entrepreneurial company with access to the resources of both parent organizations. At a news conference in 1991, shortly after the start-up of the joint venture, the General Manager outlined the goal for the venture,

We have created OCG, in fact, to ensure that we can keep pace with demands for ever-purer and more versatile electronic chemicals. The resources that we have assembled from our parent companies will not only allow us to develop innovative products; they will also allow OCG to quickly cycle them from the lab to the marketplace, and to customize them to satisfy different end-use applications.

Siecor uses Corning's Total Quality Management program. The corporate strategic emphasis is on meeting the requirements of external and internal customers "without error, on time, every time." The mission statement for one of Siecor's plants reads,

We will be the cable supplier of choice by understanding and meeting our customer's changing requirements of quality, cost, and service. This requires an eagerness to change and the ability to make rapid, continual improvement.

At Diamond Star, the orientation toward quality and continuous improvement derives from the philosophies and management styles that exist at Mitsubishi. In addition, participants in the venture recognize that to a significant degree it represents the amalgamation of two cultures. A Diamond Star brochure states,

Diamond Star represents more than an automotive venture. It is also the union of Eastern and Western cultures—a union that produced innovative methods of production and a motivated, quality-conscious work force.

Diamond Star employees are integral to building quality into the manufacturing operation. One Japanese inspection manager remarks,

Diamond Star's philosophy is that quality must be created in the [manufacturing] process. Ongoing training within [the] Quality [division] and throughout the plant, in concert with the feedback provided by our associates, creates a fine mesh, a fine sieve which blocks out defects during assembly.

ACHIEVING THE GOAL

To fulfil designated strategic objectives for the joint venture, managers and other staff are to be actively involved in processes which facilitate the realization of a Total Quality management system. In general, the cornerstones to the activation of high employee involvement systems in the joint ventures in this research encompass the following:

- *Communication systems that provide multiple forms of information and feedback to employees.* This occurs in all four joint ventures in the form of meetings, charts, telephone contacts, and written correspondence. Managers outline that if employees are well informed in the areas of product information, costs, and policies and procedures, then they are able to make better decisions, and to produce higher quality products. Feedback to employees on a variety of dimensions is important in order that they may identify areas where improvements are required. In some instances (e.g., at Mayo Forest Products and Diamond Star), this takes the form of statistical reporting. At OCG, where operations span three continents, world-wide teleconferences and meetings are used as a way to communicate among employees.
- *Education and training for employees.* These are central to providing staff with better skills in order to participate in the work environment. To facilitate and maintain flexible manufacturing systems, employees receive wide-based training. At Siecor and Diamond Star, this training enhances employee ability to rotate to various work stations and responsibilities.
- *Teamwork and a small group approach.* At Mayo Forest Products and Siecor, this may take the form of Quality Improvement Teams, Continuous Improvement Teams, and Corrective Action Teams. Siecor also functions with production work cells or minifactories. OCG operates with a number of cross-functional task teams. Quality Circle groups and "Kaizen" project teams—teams that identify improvements—exist at Diamond Star.
- *Employee rewards and recognition for their efforts and contributions to the company.* At Mayo, OCG, and Siecor, managers have created numerous incentives for employee excellence. These range from monetary rewards to T-shirts, mugs, and verbal praise. At Diamond Star, recognition is given to employees for Quality

Circle performance. At OCG (and under consideration at Siecor), rewards are offered for team performance.

In all four joint ventures, a substantial commitment of time and resources has been made in the above areas. Generally, multiple communication systems operate in the joint ventures, some more efficiently than others. Significant amounts of energy and expense have been devoted to training programs for employees, and most staff in the ventures felt that they have had sufficient training to accomplish their tasks. Systems that promote teamwork are operating in practice, although OCG and Diamond Star employees indicated there has been a reduction in time available for team-related meetings due to increased production schedules. Selection procedures for new employees aim to hire individuals with broad skills, and the ability to operate as team players.

Most JV managers take the recognition of employees seriously, and provide many tangible incentives for JV staff. Diamond Star is an exception, where recognition provided to employees is limited because of philosophical preferences on the part of the Japanese managers in the plant. In the two unionized plants, Diamond Star and Mayo Forest Products, the creation of positive union relations is thought to contribute to the effective accomplishment of company strategic objectives. Both unionized plants have taken steps to encourage a constructive union-management environment. In addition, the management at Mayo Forest Products, OCG, Siecor, and Diamond Star generally identify that the maintenance of a work environment in which employees are treated with respect and consideration is important. The mission statement for Plant 1 at Siecor outlines that employees will be "treated with dignity and respect." At Diamond Star, the employee handbook similarly describes that the company focuses on "respect for human dignity," and is interested in the creation of an environment that results in achievement and self-fulfillment.

THE RESULTS

The trend toward more participative manufacturing systems has demonstrated positive benefits. All four joint ventures excel in cost reduction, quality, and product innovation—achieved through people. A Vice-President at OCG comments,

We're way ahead of our budget in sales and profits, and it's already a very profitable business. . . . I see an enormous future for this business. I think we'll be a pretty good model to both parent companies as to a successful joint venture. I think often these things don't work out. But I think there's a real good feeling about this one.

In addition, based on the results of a questionnaire distributed in each venture, employees have a relatively high degree of job satisfaction. However, employees are more satisfied with aspects of the job related to autonomy and personal fulfillment than with actual work conditions (e.g., the implementation of company policy or supervisor competence).[1] Further, on an inventory which assessed employees' perceptions of the organizational culture, in all four JVs staff considered management to focus primarily on achievement and production demands. At Mayo Forest Products and Siecor, innovation and creativity likewise are seen as priorities in the venture.

IMPLEMENTING THE SYSTEM

The strategic philosophies and objectives for the ventures have been disseminated to employees in a variety of ways. At Mayo Forest Products the JV mission statement is frequently mentioned, and the employee newsletter is used as a vehicle to describe company objectives. Symbolism is frequently used. For example, Mayo Forest Products is described as "in the race to win" and "going for the checkered flag." "Post it" notes have been inscribed with the "team effort" slogan. At OCG, the mission statement describes the company objective to be "number one in the business." The vision for the company is communicated to employees through specific presentations on the company strategic orientation. At Siecor, the overall company mission statement is the TQM quality statement, and as such lacks a unique identity for the venture. However, Siecor's Plant 1 has created its own mission statement. At Diamond Star, mission statements are created at the company, departmental, and unit levels.

The strategic orientation for each joint venture is changing, rather than static. More specifically, at Mayo Forest Products a major reorganization occurred in 1988, eight years after the JV formation. In the case of OCG, the company is new—and managers in the joint venture are actively creating and changing policies and systems to meet novel demands in the venture. This process involves the participation of both JV and parent employees. Managers at Siecor are taking strides to reshape the manufacturing plants to operate as work cells and minifactories—a change occurring approximately 14 years after the JV was initiated. At Diamond Star, staff continue to develop new HR and managerial systems—a process complicated by the active presence of two diverse cultural groups in the operation.

The impetus for reorganization in the ventures has been largely initiated and endorsed at the executive levels. However, at multiple levels in the joint venture, various groups and individuals have actively contributed to the modifications that have been undertaken. At Mayo Forest Products, the Vice-President of the Canadian parent and the JV General Manager were responsible for a new direction in the mill. The changes at Mayo were organized in part by the consulting company, with input from a wide range of managers as well as hourly employees. Most of the reorganization at OCG was driven from the executive level of the venture, with considerable operational assistance from the HR Manager for the joint venture. At Siecor, many recent changes related to employee involvement systems began at the "grass roots" level. The management staff in the plants identified the production manager and the plant manager in Plant 1 as largely responsible. At Diamond Star, most of the systems in place have been organized at the Vice-President level of the venture, with considerable assistance from the HR department in the creation of new HR policies for the company. Many of the modifications to policy and practice at Diamond Star have their ideological base in Japanese management and production philosophies, modified to suit an American workforce.

TEAM-BASED MANUFACTURING AT SIECOR

At Siecor, where bold strides have been made toward employee involvement, a team concept was initially championed by the production manager and the plant manager in Plant 1. In 1989 equipment was reorganized and employees were identified to work on an experimental pilot team. In 1990, a second pilot team was added which was designated to operate on a permanent basis. Extensive training in employee involvement concepts and philosophy was begun. The results have been good, in terms of both employee enthusiasm and product quality. The training coordinator in the plant remarks, "it was an experiment, just to see if it [a team approach] would work with this type of environment. And it worked exceptionally well." By 1991 the management at Plant 1 had decided to reorganize the entire staff of about 600 to support the design team proposal.

The philosophy driving the team or minifactory approach is that employees work in autonomous units which are flexible and easily adaptable to product changes. The quality process remains firmly linked to the team approach. As the training coordinator at Plant 1 describes, the evolution of the team process has resulted from a desire to empower employees while at the same time enhancing product quality and company profitability. Responsibility is allocated to employees, who are called "associates" in order that they can make decisions regarding their work area. This not only includes responsibility for product completion, but for other functions that are relevant to the work team and that have traditionally been performed by management. Associates do their own work scheduling, preliminary quality checks, training, and peer reviews. New recognition programs have been developed by a team of associates. Within the next few years, associate responsibilities will expand to include hiring and firing within their work group.

Activities among the various teams are coordinated by a team project manager for production who arranges weekly meetings for associate co-ordinators on each shift. There are various associate coordinator roles: quality, site coordinator for housekeeping issues, training (e.g., scheduling and skill determination), production, and personnel (e.g., attendance, safety, and morale). Within each team, the associate coordinators are responsible for these individual areas. The project manager facilitates the meetings of coordinators from the various teams as a way of integrating and coordinating efforts across teams. For example, a coordination meeting would include the quality coordinators from all teams. This meeting offers an opportunity for coordinators to exchange ideas and information related to activities in their teams across various shifts.

In addition to the establishment of a coordinated system, teams are responsible for their own problem-solving. Continuous Improvement Teams (CITs) are in charge of improving some major function like the cables or connectors, or safety, for each shift. The CIT has its goals chartered by the Quality Improvement Team, which is comprised of the management staff at the plant. The CIT is cross-functional and has team associates working together with engineering or planning people, for example, to determine and prioritize problem areas. At Plant 1 there are two main production areas—buffering and coloring—and the CIT has members from both of these production areas on a single team. On a coloring CIT, for example, some associates from the buffering area are involved in solving problems for the coloring group in production. This would be reversed for a buffering CIT. In addition, the plants also have Corrective Action Teams (CATs) which form to work on specific problems, and once the problem is solved the CAT is disbanded. Employees are informed of CIT and CAT progress through the minutes of team meetings which are posted near the plant cafeteria. The minutes may include the team goal, modifications completed or ongoing to a production process, recommendations for changes, and projects in progress.

The keys to the effective implementation of an employee involvement system are closely related to the human resource practices operating in the plant. As the training coordinator in Plant 1 points out, training and education of employees is critical in order to communicate the goals and benefits of the new system. The plant training department takes a wide-based approach to employee education and teaches a variety of courses, including business awareness, communication skill building, group dynamics, conflict management, and group development. Related to production skills, training responsibility is gradually being handed to associates who take "train the trainer" courses and then, in turn, train other associates about work procedures. Job classification systems are under revision so there will be fewer job categories, and therefore more flexibility regarding job rotation and cross-training. Selection procedures are being modified so new employees are hired only if they have the potential to be good team members. In concert with these changes, the company is instituting new recognition systems, and eventually a revised pay system which aims to reward employees on a "pay for skills" basis. In many instances, future changes in the plant are based on outcomes from the CITs. It is a CIT that created a revised recognition system for associates in the plant.

QUALITY CIRCLES AND KAIZEN AT DIAMOND STAR MOTORS

Employees at Diamond Star are encouraged to be actively involved in the identification of problems in their respective work areas, and to create solutions to these problems through the complementary processes of quality circles and Kaizen. Quality Circle (QC) activity focuses on the specification of a problem for which there is no identified solution. An investigation is required to identify root causes to a problem, during which relevant statistical data are collected. Kaizen is part of the QC activity, and is a suggested improvement to a problem. Once an obvious solution to a problem is apparent and the benefits are defined, then the Kaizen solution can be implemented which will result in immediate improvements. In the spirit of continuous improvement, a series of Kaizen solutions can be incorporated into the QC solution.

Through the complementary process of Quality Circles and Kaizen, associates are able to suggest improvements to the manufacturing process (e.g., the reduction of defects), or introduce changes in their work environment which ultimately make their jobs easier (e.g., the use of headsets for better communication on the shop floor). The Branch Manager for Quality Circles mentions the QC emphasis is more on teamwork than on cost savings. However, the benefits to Diamond Star from QC activities are not negligible. In one instance, a QC group in the plastics shop was able to cut 73 seconds off a procedure, resulting in a one million dollar saving per shift to the company. The Branch Manager for Quality Circles works full-time with the associates to provide QC training and advice. According to him, the QC training at Diamond Star has been 100 percent adopted from the Japanese method in terms of theory, but modified to suit the American worker.

An executive from Chrysler made an interesting observation that the concepts of Quality Circles and Kaizen can operate effectively only when there is an environment of mutual trust between the associates and management. He mentions neither QCs nor Kaizen could exist in a traditional auto assembly plant. The executive elaborates that in a Chrysler factory if employees were to improve a manufacturing process, the result may be a requirement for fewer people on the line. If this were the case, the company would lay off some of its workers. At Diamond Star, associates are told there will not be layoffs—and the company is "living up to it." The Chrysler executive continues, "There's a feeling here that there's some security being built, and there's some trust. And with that goes along contribution and willingness to compete; willingness to participate from our associates that I've never seen anywhere else." He adds he has talked to various vice-presidents at Chrysler about the implementation of quality circles and Kaizen in their factories, asking "Could we ever get it in Chrysler?" He summarizes the response by stating, "Not in a million years could it ever happen. . . . You would have to take the Chrysler mentality top down and change it."

Although there have been many demonstrated successes of QC and Kaizen processes at Diamond Star, several employees and managers note there is less time for these activities than in earlier years at the plant. This has been in part the result of increased production schedules, and in part a result of a lack of commitment by all managers to a high employee involvement system. One manager remarks,

An ongoing focus on continuous improvement systems requires continuous improvement. I think where we've failed somewhere along the line a little bit with that [QC and Kaizen philosophies] is we failed to get commitment from management on those concepts. People wanted to accept that, but not knowing how to accept it, and being forced with how do you meet your production needs.

He adds he hears associates saying they want to participate in QCs and Kaizen, but their group leaders don't endorse the processes. There is now more focus on production at Diamond Star, and the company is "less people-oriented." Related to these sentiments, another manager adds,

When we started up all the philosophy, the Kaizen philosophy, the Japanese management approach to the actual workers, [it] was very highly publicized and you know it was to be implemented; it has been. But I think we stopped short in terms of training, in terms of ongoing understanding of what it's all about.

This manager believes worker involvement at Diamond Star is becoming less and less all the time. New workers receive less training in Japanese management philosophies; there is no longer Japanese cultural training offered in the orientation session, as received by the early recruits to Diamond Star.

From the associate perspective, the chairman of the bargaining committee comments, "the Kaizen system doesn't work like they [management] told everybody it would." Originally associates were told if a Kaizen project were approved, the associate would be given the opportunity to work on the project and to implement the change. But "it doesn't work that way now . . . they [management] can't afford to leave you off the line because the manpower's so short." Related to Quality Circles, this associate mentions they were supposed to have one meeting per month, but in certain manufacturing areas, this is not the case. Another associate concurs with this.

Quality circles, in the beginning I thought it was fantastic. You had the time to do it. Now as production has increased and volume is up, more people are becoming injured or calling in sick. You don't have near the time that you actually need to do a good Quality Circle project. One thing we do need is more time to work on it [QCs] if that's considered really important. But most of the things in our area that should be done in a Quality Circle, we do them automatically. If we see a change that needs to be made, we just implement it at that point. So my group probably hasn't had a Quality Circle project in probably a year.

SHIFTING ROLES FOR MANAGERS AND EMPLOYEES

The implementation of high employee involvement systems signals role shifts for both managers and employees. Management is threatened by a perceived loss of power. Workers who are now empowered with new tasks must be willing to take additional responsibility in their respective work areas. In both union and non-union environments, workers are required to adjust the "them-us" mentality of separatism in goals and objectives between workers and management. A department head at Siecor remarks,

I think the biggest challenge is getting the workforce on our side. Not opposing us. Changing how management is viewed. Instead of somebody [managers] walking around with a big stick telling you what to do, they are now people who are there enabling them [the associates] to work better, work smarter. And that's radical. That's not just radical for the plant, it's radical for management also.

As managers share power with workers, in turn production associates become more accountable for their actions. A supervisor at Siecor remarks, "a lot of the operators are hesitant to take on responsibility. They like someone else making the decisions." He adds that associates want to see tangible examples of management's intent to change operating systems—predicated on mutual trust. As a step in this direction, there are no time clocks to punch at Siecor's plants. As the personnel manager points out, "we trust them [the associates] to write down the time they work on their time card and turn it in. So for some of these folks it establishes an immediate trust that they've never felt before."

Managers feel open communication with employees is important. For example, associates at Siecor were included in a budgeting meeting with the marketing group in which sensitive financial information was shared. In addition, there is a conscious effort on the part of management to solicit employee suggestions related to the change process, and then to implement those suggestions. The department head of connectorization comments he asked some of his group to volunteer for a team to look at production capacity, and seven associates volunteered. He said some of them would have never previously volunteered for the task, and he believes employee attitudes were slowly beginning to change.

In the unionized work environment at Mayo Forest Products, management's commitment to employee involvement also was proven in practice. Employee suspicion that management meant what they said was dispelled in a variety of ways. The production supervisor comments,

Management has struggled with getting the people to accept this [participatory] way of managing. They're very suspicious about it. They don't understand why are we asking them to be involved in the decisions. They see something very suspicious about it. And as a result they don't really participate that well.

More specifically, managers at Mayo provide feedback to employees on their suggestions. Worker ideas are "passed up the line until something is done about it." In some cases the ideas are not feasible, but managers or supervisors make an effort to "get back" to each employee regarding his or her suggestion. The production supervisor adds, "the feedback part of it is the key part of the management style. . . . It doesn't really matter how ridiculous or how costly the idea is, you have to get back to the people."

The increase in the level of employee involvement in unionized mills such as at Mayo Forest Products has special implications for the traditional union-management relationship. Not everyone is comfortable with the new arrangements. The personnel administrator at Mayo Forest Products comments,

It really does create a conflict when we [management] are trying to entrust certain responsibilities and accountabilities out in the mill at the floor level. That's not traditionally done in a union environment. [In] a union environment, they are the workers and we make all the decisions as a company. And we want them to make decisions. We're looking for added value from our lumber and we want them [the workers] to be accountable for the grades. . . . We are entrusting that responsibility to them. We get a little conflict from that because that's not traditionally what they want to do. They just want to do their jobs and go home at night. So there's conflict with the new style of management and the traditional [style] of what would be perceived as a union employee's role.

Some workers are very willing to accept the additional responsibilities, others are not. The production supervisor at Mayo notes a majority of the unionized employees are in favor of greater employee involvement. He comments,

We have a lot of people who see what we're trying to do and they're helping us. We'll run this place almost as a cooperative between management and union. That will be a turning point for us. We're getting close.

To signal commitment to employee involvement, a union employee participated on the hiring panel for recruitment of 30 new employees to the mill. This was an important step toward increasing the union's involvement in decision-making in the mill.

Part of the difficulty in instituting the performance management system at Mayo Forest Products revolves around a shift in power and control from management and supervisory staff to unionized employees. Referring to middle managers, the General Manager comments, "they feel they're giving up their authority or their control and that scares me—because obviously they still don't understand all the principles that we're working with." To facilitate openness of the part of supervisors to share power, a consulting group was hired to train supervisors regarding the goals of high employee involvement systems. Training focuses on communication skills, setting up self-managing work teams, and the supervisor's role as coach and facilitator in this process.

LESSONS LEARNED

The unusual degree of similarity between the strategic objectives of these four international joint ventures signals a message to managers of what progressive companies are implementing to ensure corporate successes. The emphasis in the companies is solidly in the following areas:

1. employee involvement in which teamwork, "ownership" of responsibilities, and continuous problem-solving are encouraged;
2. extensive communication systems that inform employees about how they are doing, as well as provide information related to company strategy and goals;
3. education and training in broad skills;
4. a wide range of meaningful rewards and recognition for employees who excel;
5. treating employees with dignity and respect;
6. flexibility and a willingness to reorganize systems when necessary;
7. obtaining "buy in" from employees at various levels in order to legitimize change processes.

NOTE

1. Refer to Appendix 3 for questionnaire results for all four joint ventures.

PART II

Management of the Joint Venture–Parent Relationship

CHAPTER 4

Parent Goals and
Strategic HRM

The most important thing on the human resource side is to determine
how similar or dissimilar the partner is that you're going to partner
with. Clearly, as I feel the concerns of employees, the concerns are
minimized when the partner that you're getting is very much like you.
In areas where it's dissimilar, I think a lot of these issues bubble up
around just uncertainty and are translated into problems of job security.

Manager, OCG

A key feature of progressive joint ventures is the accomplishment of strategic initiatives through optimal utilization of human resources. However,
in most cases attention is not given to the "type" of joint venture which
exists, or, more specifically, to how HRM can complement or enhance JV
goals in relation to respective parent roles. Of the four joint ventures in
this investigation, two are "specialized" and the parents have separate
responsibilities; the other two ventures are "value-added" and the parents
have joint roles in the accomplishment of JV objectives. The form of joint
venture has implications for how HRM policy and practice operates, especially in relation to the transfer of technology. For example, in value-
added joint ventures in which both parents contribute product-related
expertise, technology can be transferred between the parents and the venture through staff exchanges or extensive communication networks. In
specialization joint ventures, parent input to the venture may be more
one-sided. Related to parent roles, whether the parents share or dominate
in the management responsibilities for the joint venture also influences
HR policy and practice.

In international joint ventures, considerable attention typically is given to how the parent firms complement each other in terms of strategic or technological factors. Another important but little discussed issue in international JVs is the extent to which the corporate cultures and value systems between the JV parent firms are compatible. According to JV managers, complementary parent values are a critical but overlooked component of corporate venturing, which in significant and subtle ways contributes to JV success in the human resources area. When parent corporate cultures and values are relatively similar, fewer adjustments are required of parent employees transferred to the venture. Otherwise, JV transferees may experience stress and uncertainty related to JV policies, values, and operating norms.

Successful management of staff relationships, both in the JV and between the JV and parents, contributes to strategic outcomes in the joint ventures. Exemplary personal skills, maintaining credibility with a variety of organizational stakeholders, and development of trust are all considered by managers as important to the effective transfer of information and skills. Despite this fact, training for managers in interorganizational management skills is neglected.

JOINT VENTURE TYPES

Joint ventures are formed for different purposes, and subsequently partner roles will vary depending on desired strategic outcomes. As one form of categorization, Lei and Slocum (1991) distinguished between "specialization" and "value-added" joint ventures. Accordingly, in specialization ventures, each partner contributes distinctive competencies in a particular area or activity (e.g., one produces, the other markets). This form of JV is likely to be organized around defined functions or roles. In value-added joint ventures, the partners actively contribute expertise and information that results in novel outcomes which neither partner might achieve alone (e.g., both parents are involved in joint design or production).

Both Mayo Forest Products and Diamond Star are examples of a "specialization" international joint venture. In the case of Mayo Forest Products, the roles of each of the parent companies are well determined. Mitsubishi is responsible for marketing 85 percent of the lumber product to Japan. Pacific Forest Products handles marketing to other destinations, ensures a steady supply of raw resources in the form of logs, and has management responsibility for the mill. The management groups of both parent companies perceive they benefit from this arrangement, and that each is able to contribute complementary ability and competency to the success of Mayo Forest Products. Primarily, Mitsubishi provides the joint venture with market access and distribution networks in Japan; Pacific Forest Products contributes raw lumber resources to the venture.

Likewise, at Diamond Star the roles of each parent are defined specifically. The benefit to Mitsubishi is clear. The Japanese multinational gains entry to the American market, and has access to Chrysler's distribution networks for the marketing and promotion of products in the United States. In turn, Mitsubishi brings advanced technology and its manufacturing and management style to the plant. In addition to marketing networks, Chrysler brings to the joint venture experience in dealing with an American workforce and practices. Originally, an objective at Chrysler was to have several of its managers transfer to Diamond Star in order to have exposure to, and learn from, the Japanese methods. In reality, this objective did not materialize to the degree Chrysler management had hoped, and within a couple of years into the venture, approximately half of the assigned Chrysler managers returned to the parent firm. With the return of many managers from Diamond Star to Chrysler (initiated by the American partner), the opportunity for Chrysler staff to learn new procedures and techniques was automatically reduced. In addition, the financial benefits of the union were less obvious to Chrysler, especially because some of Diamond Star's automobile products were in competition with Chrysler's own models.

OCG and Siecor are examples of "value-added" international joint ventures. The partners have independent expertise in related areas, and each can benefit from the union which the joint venture provides. At OCG, the photoresist business of Olin is combined in a complementary way with the photoresist and polyimide businesses of Ciba-Geigy. At Siecor, the cable development technology of Siemens is combined with the optical fiber expertise of Corning. These ventures provide the partners with the opportunity to share both the risks and costs required to compete in high development-cost industries. Although the potential for technology loss from one parent to the other exists, this concern is balanced with the possibility of gains in the international marketplace. At both OCG and Siecor, the parent and JV managers felt the union is worthwhile. These venture partnerships have already attained greater product excellence in the particular JV market sector than either parent could attain alone.

Further, Killing (1983: 16-22) categorized joint ventures as operating under three different management styles: dominant parent JVs, shared management ventures, and independent ventures. Dominant joint ventures are staffed entirely by one parent and "managed by their dominant parents virtually as if they were wholly-owned subsidiaries." The "board of directors, although containing executives from each parent, plays a largely ceremonial role." Alternately, Killing described a shared management venture as one in which "both parents play a meaningful managerial role." The board or executive committee is likely to have real influence, the partners share technical or product expertise, and both parents have an active role in the decision-making required for the joint venture. In independent joint ventures the general manager has autonomy for making decisions that affect the joint venture, without need for recourse to a JV board.

JV PARENT ROLES AND HRM

Although a shared role between the parents exists in all the joint ventures in this investigation, it is most apparent in the value-added joint ventures. This has implications for HRM. In value-added ventures, in human resources as well as in other areas, contributions and inputs to the joint venture are generally made by *both* parents. At both OCG and Siecor, although one parent was assigned management responsibility for the joint venture, both parents are involved in transferring managerial and technological expertise to the joint venture. This is accomplished, for example, through:

- staffing key positions in the JV from both parents;
- encouraging employee transfers between the JV and both parents;
- extensive communication linkages in the JV and between the JV and both parents; and
- rewards for innovation and technological achievements.

More specifically, a primary goal for OCG and Siecor is to achieve product innovation and quality based on complementary parent expertise. To accomplish this objective, technology sharing between the parents is a priority and is accomplished through strategic HRM initiatives. At OCG, senior JV Vice-Presidents are chosen to represent both parent firms. The biggest issue for the venture, the transfer of a minority group of employees from the Swiss parent into the JV, was initiated to acquire parent expertise in research and development (R&D). Further, a "no-bid back" policy was instituted to retain the technological talent in OCG until the JV stabilized. Reward incentives were developed for technological accomplishments. Finally, various intercontinental communication systems have been set up to facilitate sharing of information and technology among JV and parent groups.

At Siecor, product innovation and quality are also enhanced through numerous transfers and permanent staff relocations between the joint venture and the parents. Many of the senior executives in the production area at Siecor were relocated from the American parent Corning, and brought knowledge related to optical fibers with them. Cable expertise was introduced to Siecor through transfers between the joint venture and the German parent. In the latter instance, technology was transferred by Siemens employees who were temporarily relocated to Siecor in the R&D

division. Parent goals of quality enhancement were encouraged in training programs, by the employee performance review process, and by reward and recognition programs for innovative technical accomplishments.

In contrast, Mayo and Diamond Star are shared joint ventures (both parents have separate but important roles related to marketing versus production), but in each case one of the partners is more dominant (e.g., Pacific Forest Products, Mitsubishi). At both Mayo and Diamond Star, the parent with the management contract took the lead in providing administrative *and* technological expertise to the venture. At Diamond Star, there is some involvement by Chrysler, but this is very minimal. Mitsubishi provides influence and expertise to the joint venture through numerous staff assignments to the venture, and through transfers of Diamond Star staff to Japan in order to transfer to the venture information and technology related to Mitsubishi management and manufacturing style.

At Mayo Forest Products, where parent roles are specialized with minimal requirements for technology transfer, staff exchanges do not occur between the joint venture and the parents. At Mayo, communication networks with either parent are relatively limited; however, communication occurs with both parents through the JV board and advisory committee.

PARTNER COMPATIBILITY

When JV partners lack well-aligned strategic intents, then long-term venture success is likely to be tenuous. As Lorange and Roos (1991) suggested, the strategic match of the partners is critical. Not only must the parties to the venture complement each other, but it is important that they don't infringe on each other's territory. It helps if there is cultural similarity. Typically, JV partners consider how similar or complementary their strategic objectives are related to competitive product development or marketing prior to venture start-up. Much less often is the match of corporate values and philosophy related to HRM strategies between the partners evaluated. According to a manager at OCG, this is a serious omission, especially when disparity between the values and objectives of the parents results in employee stress and uncertainty.

At Siecor and OCG, partner compatibility (e.g., similar objectives, complementary corporate culture, aligned expectation for the JV) is important. In particular, this suggests:

- parent firms should seek out partners with complementary goals and objectives;
- managers should be aware of both JV and parent objectives; and
- HR managers should be involved in the early planning to ensure a strategic role and to assist in the "integration process" between the JV and parents.

Related to these considerations, if the parents are to achieve optimal realization of their goals, then one might expect the parent goals to be in close alignment. At Mayo, OCG, and Siecor, the parents have basically the same philosophy for how the joint venture can achieve the strategic mandate. Managers in the joint venture contribute to this process, as does the JV management board.

Alternately, Mitsubishi and Chrysler operate their own automobile plants differently from one another. One Diamond Star manager remarked, "the Americans are going to support their corporate culture . . . and the Japanese want to support their corporate culture or their beliefs of how they think Diamond Star should be run." With regard to quality and employee involvement, Mitsubishi has a similar orientation to the other parent companies in this investigation; traditionally Chrysler has not focused on either quality management or employee involvement to the same extent.

When the intents or corporate initiatives of the parents are dissimilar, employees may be confused regarding expected behaviors or operating values in the venture. Related to this form of corporate disparity, a production employee at Diamond Star indicated,

The problem we're finding out, you have the Japanese management on one side, the Chrysler management on the other, and they don't communicate and so what comes down to you are two different views of the same thing. . . . The Japanese expect you to do a good job. And you don't have that same expectation with the American managers.

Not only are employees uncertain regarding organizational priorities in this instance, but a further consideration is how loyalty within the joint venture may be fractured as a result of obvious differences in parent norms or values. Although loyalty was not a particular problem at Diamond Star, if the majority of employees in a joint venture identify with the parent from the same national or corporate culture, managers from the second parent may be at a distinct disadvantage gaining commitment from the workforce.

At OCG, where a minority group of employees was merged into the venture from the Swiss parent firm, managers felt similar corporate cultures, and knowledge of the culture and objectives of both parents helped to integrate employees into the joint venture. For example, both Olin and Ciba-Geigy have a history of supporting employee contributions through well-developed reward and benefit programs. Not only did parent value similarity facilitate the creation of HR policy for the joint venture in this area, but it also reduced the adjustments required of employees in order to fit into a new system.

JV RELATIONSHIP MANAGEMENT

The effective management of relationships, both in the joint venture and between the joint venture and parents, appears to be a critical factor to JV success. In all of the joint ventures, personal skills and the ability of managers to facilitate good relationships between the parents and the joint venture, and within the joint venture, are considered important. Patience, openness, trust, and objectivity in dealing with multiple stakeholders were mentioned by managers as desirable qualities. This implies managers respond to the priorities of various stakeholder groups in each venture (e.g., union-management, R&D and production, employees transferred to the joint venture, or diverse cultural groups).

The general manager at Mayo Forest Products suggests that managers require "a good understanding of the politics of the business," and must avoid playing one partner against the other. Concerning relationships between JV managers and managers in the parent firms, the General Manager at Mayo mentions the development of trust is also important. He states, "I would always wear the Mayo hat and was always very direct with them [the Mitsubishi representatives]. Always very up front with them and very consistent. I was never deceitful, never lied. Always went at them with the same story. And we [the JV staff] got the results." A Vice-President at Pacific Forest Products notes a great deal of time is required to make the JV-parent relationship successful. He adds, "It was important to me to get to know all of the people in the whole process, from the most senior individual to everybody that was involved in the marketing of the products for Mayo."

At OCG, a manager noted when you are working with people from different backgrounds and approaches in the parent firms, it is critical to understand different styles and motivations. He adds that in joint ventures, a manager needs "to maximize what you can do yourself and what you have your parents do for you. So your managers who will be successful, I think, have to understand their own culture, both parent cultures, and where they can make use of them." This statement implicitly suggests managers need a broad understanding of all strategic players linked to the venture, and how tasks might best be accomplished. Similarly, at Siecor one manager notes that credibility is important, as well as sufficient business knowledge to ask appropriate questions of members of both parents. Finally, at Diamond Star many managers mention the importance of being able to bridge cross-cultural differences through enhanced knowledge and communication. In all the ventures, the establishment of personal relationships between senior executives in the parents and in the joint venture contributes to development of informal channels of communication through which information can be exchanged and tasks accomplished.

Further, in each of the joint ventures, the identification of needs and building of commitment are accomplished in different ways. For example, the inclusion of a union representative on the selection committee at Mayo was a step toward involving the union in the mill operation. At OCG, the HR manager first determined the needs of former parent employees before developing new HR policy. At Siecor, managers demonstrated to production employees they "meant what they said" about generating greater employee involvement at the plants. At Diamond Star, some managers in the HR department saw themselves in a balancing role between various groups in the plant (e.g., union-management, Japanese-American). New HR policy was created at Diamond Star only after consultation with American and Japanese managers. In all joint ventures, a focus on communication encourages various groups to express concerns or offer suggestions. In these ways managers become more familiar with issues of importance to employees, and are able to offer acceptable solutions to problems when they arise.

In descriptions by JV managers of how the venture-parent relationship might operate, the establishment of trust and credibility, as well as an understanding of the operating styles and motivations of various groups is mentioned. Although not present in the joint ventures in this study, to ideally encourage JV-parent cooperation:

- rewards could be offered for managers who reinforce JV-parent cooperation;
- training could be given in international management and intercompany dynamics; and
- performance reviews could emphasize goals that are set for intercompany cooperation.

In none of the joint ventures did managers either request or get training, information, or rewards to enhance interorganizational aspects of the JV-parent relationship. Given the importance many managers attach to the development of personal relationships with managers in the partner companies, joint training sessions that include members of both the joint venture and the parents might facilitate not only relationship building, but also the exchange of information related to key issues, concerns, and ideas. Further, when parent groups are from diverse cultures, training to facilitate cross-cultural understanding might also be enhanced.

LESSONS LEARNED

The management of the JV-parent relationship is a critical, yet overlooked aspect of how joint ventures can be organized to be most successful. Depending on the form of joint venture (e.g., specialization or value-added) HRM operates differently. In value-added joint ventures,

HRM policy helps to facilitate the contributions of both parents to create management and technological synergy. This is accomplished through:

- staffing the JV from both parents
- numerous transfers from both parents
- extensive communication networks
- rewards for technological accomplishments

In specialization joint ventures, where the parent roles remain more separate, there is less need for coordination across the parent and JV firms.

Partner compatibility is important. Ideally partners will have similar objectives, complementary corporate cultures, and aligned expectations for the joint venture. The complexity of the interorganizational relationships between the joint venture and parents requires special qualities of managers. In particular, managers need to be able to interface between multiple stakeholders as part of a trust-building process.

CHAPTER 5

Joint Venture Autonomy or Interdependence

It's probably true to say that from a general standpoint the number of parent employees that are brought in [to the joint venture] probably has a big influence on how, and how fast the joint venture grows, what it looks like, and what kind of culture it has.

Manager, Siecor

Whether the joint ventures are value-added or specialized, at Mayo Forest Products, OCG, Siecor, and Diamond Star each set of parents has specified roles to fulfil as part of the formal JV agreement. In many cases, these roles are shared. However, related to the allocation of management responsibility, in each joint venture *one* parent is assigned the "management contract" for the venture. Although there are benefits to be gained from this arrangement (e.g., ability to easily draw from established HR policy or materials), there are also inherent problems. For instance, the parent with the management contract will often infuse the JV with its own policies and operating style, either intentionally or unintentionally. Implicitly this gives the managing parent greater influence and control of the venture. As time goes on, the assignment of the management contract to one parent may not be entirely acceptable to the non-managing parent, especially when changes in strategy for the joint venture are desired. Although the parents may both have managerial expertise to offer the joint venture, to some extent parent offerings are curtailed when management responsibility is formally assigned to a single parent.

Related to predominance by one parent in the venture, there are implications for whether the joint venture has a separate identity, or is simply

a version of the managing parent company. In some instances JV autonomy is hampered when large numbers of parent staff and the use of one
parent's resources restrict the development of policy and practice unique
to the requirements of the venture. Parent influence in the joint venture
is especially noticeable in HR policy and procedures, when strategy and
values are transferred into the joint venture through training, salary structures, or performance review systems that mirror HR systems in the parent
firm.

THE JV MANAGEMENT CONTRACT

Three of the joint ventures in this investigation share 50/50 equity ownership between the parents, and have an equally shared JV board structure. Mayo Forest Products is the exception, with a 60/40 equity split in
favor of Pacific Forest Products, with an extra Pacific Forest Products
member on the JV board. However, in all four joint ventures, one parent
was given responsibility for management in the venture by virtue of assignment of the management contract. This allocation of responsibility
was decided early in the JV formation, except at Mayo where the management contract was assigned to Pacific Forest Products at the time of
the reorganization in 1988. In all instances, the parent with the management contract draws on its own resources in the management of the venture. At Mayo Forest Products HR policies for salaried staff are adopted
from Pacific Forest Products. The decision by OCG's partners to grant
Olin Corporation the management contract was partly related to the large
percentage of Olin employees who were absorbed into the venture. Further, OCG was in the start-up phase of its operation, and many new HR
policies were being quickly implemented in the venture. As a result, OCG
managers decided to hasten the policy development process through the
initial adoption of HR policies from Olin. The Quality program and related performance review process were adapted from the American parent; training for OCG employees was done primarily in the extensive Olin
training facility. The newsletter currently distributed to employees in the
venture was a product created for all Olin operations.

At Siecor, the parents have a balanced management arrangement:
Corning manages the joint venture in the United States location, and
Siemens has the management contract for a jointly shared joint venture
in Germany. HR staff at Siecor have many linkages with their counterparts
at Corning. Training content and the reward systems for salaried staff at
Siecor are very similar to those found in the parent firm. In addition, the
strategic focus at Siecor is derived largely from policy directives used at
Corning.

The upper ranks of the joint venture are staffed primarily by former
Corning managers. Related to this, much of the focus on total quality

manufacturing and employee involvement systems in the manufacturing plants was introduced to Siecor through the Corning connection. Alternately, Siemens primarily provides the joint venture with technical advice and training on new equipment.

In the area of human resource management, managers have mixed opinions as to how much influence on policy and practice should be derived from Corning, and how much of HR functioning should be created for the individual requirements of Siecor. One senior manager, who feels there is a significant influence from Corning, comments,

There's a much stronger influence on our organization by Corning than there is by Siemens, and Corning has a value structure that they make a strong effort of disseminating down through all parts of their organization. . . . But when it comes to passing on information and systems issues, there does occur a lot of conflict in the sense that there are times when within the [Siecor] organization it is perceived that Corning is trying to impose their particular HR systems on us. Not for our benefit, but for theirs.

Another manager at Siecor adds there is a benefit to Siecor in being able to absorb or adapt HR policies from a parent company. He explains it is less costly to use materials originally produced at Corning which are already prepared, and well conceived. In his view, Corning does not put any pressure on Siecor to use its HR policies. HR staff at Corning operate in a support role and provide assistance at the request of the management at Siecor. An HR manager mentions much of the influence on personnel policies is derived from the quality focus central to operations at Corning. This individual notes, "Corning has said, and rightfully so, that we expect Siecor to introduce, implement, and adhere to the whole quality process the same as Corning does. Now did that have to be 'forced on us,' the answer is no."

At Diamond Star, both the management and the manufacturing focus for the plant are taken from Mitsubishi. For example, Diamond Star has a "just-in-time" production system and operates using Kaizen to facilitate the continuous improvement of work processes. Employees are cross-trained in various jobs and rotate to different manufacturing tasks. Senior management at the plant has instituted a no layoff policy for staff and has adhered to this decision. There are morning exercises for employees; uniforms are mandatory on the shop floor and optional for office staff. Quality circles, the union-management philosophy, staffing, reward, and training initiatives, have all been largely adapted from the Japanese parent. According to an employee on a task team from the American parent, the group had been told to "assist Mitsubishi, but not to run the plant." In the HR area, staff have created modified policies which suit the styles and philosophies of an American workforce. For instance, training in quality circles was adapted to better suit American workers. Although the Japanese do not usually favor recognition programs, consideration was given to the implementation of such programs to meet the expectation of American workers that good work deserves to be recognized.

PARENT INFLUENCE IN THE VENTURE

Although JV managers may adopt policies and methods from either parent, strategic or cultural influences will be stronger from the managing parent firm (e.g., the parent with the management contract). As Frayne and Geringer (1989) speculated, the extent of overall parent involvement in the venture related to the placement, quality, and number of staff; training content; form of performance appraisal; and type of compensation and reward can be expected to affect the JV corporate culture and identity. In addition, the content and type of communication systems which operate in the joint venture, and between the joint venture and the parents, are related to the degree to which employees of the joint venture form an affiliation to the venture company as opposed to either of the parent firms.

At OCG, for example, where communication to the venture is largely from Olin, one executive from Ciba-Geigy questions whether employees feel more like a subsidiary of Olin than a stand alone joint venture. The employee handbook distributed to OCG staff was originally produced for the American parent and describes Olin philosophies and benefits. The monthly employee newsletter is produced for Olin organizations, including OCG. Related to the predominant influence at OCG of Olin on how communication channels operate, a manager from Ciba-Geigy observes,

It was never in my recollection discussed who would be the main communication partner or would we both [communicate with OCG]. So it seems as though Olin, because they were to provide the services, had found a way to wrap OCG into their network of communications about general Olin information. On the other hand Ciba-Geigy does, I think, nothing to wrap them in on this side. The idea I thought strategically at the outset was to have all these employees [at OCG] feel like a stand alone venture. My belief is the Olin strategy of wrapping them into their newspaper is going to have them feeling longer term like a subsidiary of the Olin Corporation . . . and not an equal partner with Ciba-Geigy.

Although there is an additional cost in producing a newsletter for OCG, one manager notes there may also be some benefits related to the creation of a more secure identity for employees in the joint venture. A manager at Ciba-Geigy suggests there is merit in the publication of a separate newsletter for OCG that incorporates items from both parent newsletters when they are relevant and affect OCG.

In the best interests of the joint venture, and related to strategic HRM objectives, the parents must decide the level of JV autonomy versus dependence on parent policy that is desirable. Ideally, consideration is given to the effect on the joint venture of an infusion of readily available management services into the venture, versus the creation of innovative HR policy unique to JV needs. For instance, in an entrepreneurial venture like OCG, a simple adoption of policy from either larger parent firm is likely to be inappropriate to the demands of the much faster paced market in which OCG competes.

To elaborate, the parents have ready-made, usually high-quality materials and programs to which JV management can have access. This is especially useful in the start-up phase of an operation when the creation of a multitude of new policies and processes is required. The development of new systems is likely to demand considerable staff time and energy, and be more expensive. However, if there is an overreliance of parent materials and systems in the joint venture, the venture may inappropriately mirror the parent culture, with little focus on unique JV requirements. If the joint venture is structured to be qualitatively different from the parents (e.g., to be entrepreneurial as at OCG) rather than large and bureaucratic (as tends to be the case in the parent corporations), then a simple adoption of the same strategies and HR policies as the parents is unlikely to meet the specific demands of the venture.

Although to some extent it is easier to coordinate the strategic and HR processes in the venture if one parent is the primary source of input, this assumes the second parent has little to offer to the joint venture in terms of HRM or strategic policy. For example, in the early stages of the JV negotiations at OCG, management responsibility for the venture was clearly designated to Olin. The contractual agreement to lease management services from Olin was not entirely satisfactory to all Ciba-Geigy executives. Senior members from the Ciba-Geigy side of the operation realized they had very little management control in a business in which they are a 50/50 partner.

An OCG Vice-President who came from Ciba-Geigy observes that even before the joint venture was formed, there was concern that the Swiss parent wanted to be more than a financial investor. Originally Ciba-Geigy wanted to "really have an equal voice in the management and the operation of the company." This same individual, who had considerable experience in the benefits area, hoped his expertise would be called upon when determining a new benefits package for employees at OCG.

The Vice-President for Human Resources of Ciba-Geigy United States notes that by contracting services for OCG from Olin, he had neither funding nor personnel built into his departmental HR budget to formally contribute to the OCG venture. Subsequently, he took a "back door" approach to reviewing HR policies for possible implementation at OCG.

Although this Ciba-Geigy executive added he will eagerly review policies as requested, the question remained as to the level of involvement which was reasonable and appropriate for him, given the management contract for OCG was formally assigned to the American parent.

Despite concern there is insufficient influence from Ciba-Geigy in the management of OCG, the contractual arrangement was generally viewed as satisfactory. One executive comments,

My initial reaction was sort of negative, in that I thought it would be better if OCG had its own people providing financial and HR systems . . . and I just had my doubts that some service arrangement might not work out well. But it's turned out that generally these groups have performed quite well for us, and I think they like working for OCG in a sense. . . . On the plus side it permits OCG to be a fairly lean organization in that it doesn't have levels of bureaucracy and all these support groups on our payroll directly.

Related to assignment of the management contract, it is likely to be advantageous for the partners to consider how the expertise of managers in the parent firm not assigned the contract might also contribute to the venture. If the second parent in fact chooses to be involved in the joint venture, then participation could be structured by the formation of joint task forces in the HR area (as was done at OCG). In addition, allocation of funds to the second parent for its contributions, or temporary assignment of personnel from the second parent to the joint venture, may contribute long-term benefits to the venture. In this way, the parent that is not officially assigned the management contract for the joint venture neither abdicates responsibility in providing expertise to the joint venture, nor feels uninvited if contributions are offered.

In summary, the parent with primary responsibility for management in the joint venture is in a position to broadly influence the corporate culture and HRM practices which operate in the venture. This may occur by adopting parent newsletters in the venture, or by training employees with parent materials in a parent training facility, for example. Further, the presence of a large number of parent executives unavoidably infuses a joint venture with the norms and values of the parent executives. Accordingly, in early JV negotiations the implications of the assignment of the management contract on the development of the corporate culture in the joint venture should be considered. Depending on the goals for the venture, there may be advantages if both parents contribute corporate values and expertise.

PARAMETERS FOR JOINT VENTURE AUTONOMY

Although at a strategic level, many JV goals and objectives are directed by the parent firms, at the operations level JV managers are generally given greater independence as to how to run the operation to meet strategic goals. JV managers suggest the level of autonomy given the joint venture was related to the success of the venture in meeting parent expectations. In support of this assumption, Killing (1983) noted that if the joint venture is operating in a manner considered successful by members of the parent firms, then JV managers are given relative independence. Killing concluded that autonomy in the venture both results from good performance, and leads to improved performance. The ability of JV managers to effectively interface with the parents is important, and the development of trust between the joint venture and the parents contributes to independence of the ventures.

The managers of various departments of the joint ventures surveyed did not take their independence from the parents for granted. This finding is supported by a senior HR executive at Siecor who remarks that one of the major challenges for the HR department was to maintain excellence in order to avoid intervention from the parents. This manager states,

In the area of personnel and people, I want to keep our company as good as it can be. I feel that if I do not, that I could have some intervention from my parents. So if I think about that as a challenge, and I think if you talked to our financial people, they would tell you the same thing.

Further, a plant manager at Siecor notes that despite welcomed assistance provided by the parent companies, the joint venture strives for autonomy. He adds, "I don't ever remember it being written down, but the sense you got being here was that it was the intention that we would strive to be autonomous. And that was the direction we headed." Members of the management staff explain they have learned and benefited from the associations with the parent companies—a relationship which has changed over time. A Director at Siecor remarks that in the beginning, the technology for the venture was supplied by Siemens and the fiber product by Corning. Now Siecor is at the point where "we've manufactured so much more cable than Siemens that we're in a position of teaching and learning." He adds this is "an interesting by-product of the relationship. Nobody anticipated it."

At Diamond Star, where there is considerable influence from the Japanese, many employees identify more with the Japanese parent than with the joint venture. One manager notes, "the day-to-day visibility of Chrysler is very low." Another manager explains, "almost everything that goes on here [at Diamond Star] has a Japanese influence to it . . . this has always been a Japanese-run company, always will be." Related to these comments, one Japanese manager hints it may be time for Diamond Star to create a more autonomous identity. He suggests that now most employees at Diamond Star understand "the Japanese way of business, Japanese thought, and the Japanese way of production. And in time, they have to realize and to decide to think their own way; the Diamond Star way they have to create." A manager of the Chrysler task force mentions that in the engineering area, they "try to let the parents do their own thing and to keep them out of any day-to-day operations of Diamond Star. Diamond Star is like a separate autonomous child from the two parents. And it's tough, but it's very important not to let any parent matters get to the smaller [JV] company."

The development of JV autonomy is related to an ability on the part of parent employees to focus on the development of the joint venture as a successful and separate entity. Initially some managers found this difficult, especially if they felt their primary ties were to the parent firm. At Diamond Star, a senior manager who is a Chrysler employee mentions that originally his "sole purpose" was to learn Japanese manufacturing methods and to transfer these methods to Chrysler. His feelings changed over time. He remarks,

Now it seems like you want to try and be part of the team and make Diamond Star successful. And I hear very little from Chrysler anymore, being honest about it. We're so tied up in what we're doing here to make Diamond Star successful; and not Chrysler or Mitsubishi, but [to make] Diamond Star successful. So I think we pretty well feel like we're on the Diamond Star team.

Another Chrysler employee at Diamond Star comments, "there was always an unwritten mission statement that our efforts would be to help Diamond Star." Further, managers realize the necessity of setting aside parent agendas that might negatively affect the joint venture. One manager remarks, "your own hidden agendas, you've got to put aside. You can't go into a joint venture saying, 'I'm going to make one of the parents stronger.'" Employees who were not interested in nurturing the venture's success generally left the joint venture early to return to the parent firm.

The General Manager at Mayo Forest Products was told by the Pacific Forest Products executive most involved in the joint venture to manage his business unit and make changes as required at the operations level. However, the development of an autonomously functioning joint venture was made difficult by the strong presence of the Canadian partner in the strategic direction for the mill. One employee at Mayo volunteered he worked for Pacific Forest Products and added, "everybody here works for Pacific Forest Products. If someone at Pacific Forest Products is not happy with your performance, then you don't have a job. If somebody at Mitsubishi is not happy about your performance, they have to live with it." Another employee notes that he feels Mayo Forest Products is treated like a division of Pacific Forest Products. In fact, frequent performance com-

parisons are made by managers in the mill between the Mayo operation
and other Pacific Forest Products mills in the area.

Within the network of relationships that tie Mayo to Pacific Forest Products, a senior manager at Pacific Forest Products reflects,

In the management of it [Mayo] we manage it not appreciably different than our
other sawmills. And when I say that we have a manager there and while he's a
Mayo Forest Products general manager, I personally view him in the same way as
I do the general manager of our other sawmills. He conceivably might have a little
bit more latitude in that he serves two masters, not just one.

The reporting link for Mayo is to the Canadian parent; subsequently
the JV general manager at Mayo requires approval from Pacific Forest
Products before making certain decisions, such as in the areas of staffing
and compensation practices. In all instances, approval is required before
hiring anyone and for allocating salary increases. The general manager
finds this situation frustrating and remarks, "It's prevented me from doing
a proper job of recognizing my staff. It's prevented us from doing a proper
job of organizing the staff as things change and evolve. We've done a poor
job of properly compensating people." Lack of autonomy may force managers into political action. At Mayo Forest Products, this took the form of
an informal system for staffing. The general manager explains that to
accomplish some of his goals, he has some unapproved positions on the
payroll under which some people are being paid on an hourly basis under
a "hidden payroll."

THE CREATION OF A SEPARATE JV IDENTITY

Despite the influence of Pacific Forest Products, the general manager
at Mayo has been able to make a variety of changes which he felt were
necessary to upgrade the mill and to create a new management style. At
the mill site there are no visible signs Mayo Forest Products is related to
Pacific Forest Products. The general manager at Mayo comments, "we
have our own corporate identity, our own colors, our own policy manuals.
Let's take advantage of that."

In the other joint ventures in this investigation, similar steps have been
taken by JV managers to create a corporate culture and practices. Within
the joint venture environment, new corporate goals were developed following methods used by wholly-owned companies. These strategies are
well documented in the literature on corporate culture change in organizations (e.g., Badaracco and Ellsworth, 1989; Frost et al., 1985; Joiner,
1987; Killmann and Covin, 1988; Kouzes and Posner, 1987; Morgan, 1988;
Schein, 1984; Walton and Lawrence, 1985). Related to how corporate

values were introduced at Mayo, OCG, Siecor, and Diamond Star, this included:

- mission statements unique to the joint venture (at Mayo, OCG, and Diamond Star; at Siecor this occurs at the plant level);
- a vision statement repeated to employees through verbal and written communication (all four joint ventures);
- a company newsletter that focuses on JV issues and activities (Mayo, Siecor, Diamond Star);
- communication systems designed to link multiple JV locations (OCG, Siecor);
- staffing that focuses on selection of employees to suit the requirements of the venture (all four joint ventures);
- training that is aligned to strategic objectives of the venture (all four joint ventures);
- recognition and reward for performance which exemplifies corporate values of quality and innovation (Mayo, OCG, Siecor, and Diamond Star for QC accomplishments); and
- performance review that recognizes quality, teamwork, and employee involvement (OCG, Siecor, Diamond Star).

Alternately, certain features of joint ventures make the consistent communication and application of corporate values and norms problematic. For example, multiple locations for OCG both within the United States as well as in Europe and Japan present some integration difficulties, despite communication systems specifically designed to alleviate this situation. Further, the presence of subgroups (e.g., union-management; supervisors-production employees; R&D-production) in the ventures, each group with its own distinct value systems, contributes to varied interpretations by employees of how the company strategic goals should operate. Multiple languages (especially at Diamond Star), the relatively large size of the company (Siecor, Diamond Star), and the level of commitment to information sharing and involvement (all four joint ventures) likewise determine the degree to which values and norms are communicated throughout the venture.

In order to create an environment in which cultural changes may evolve, JV managers focus on instituting philosophical changes *in practice.* At Mayo Forest Products and Siecor, plant managers mentioned they aim to "do what they say," and to use overt demonstrations that they desire employee involvement. Employee suggestions are used to modify operations, and some managers mentioned that they specifically tried to reward and recognize employees for their contributions. When managers persist in the consistent reinforcement of the norms and values of a revised corporate system, then over time one might expect employee concerns about realized changes to eventually be dispelled. Open communication and reward and recognition that reinforce revised corporate philosophies assisted employees in the ventures in better understanding new operating values and requirements.

LESSONS LEARNED

The parent with the management contract draws heavily on its own resources in the management and coordination of the venture. In the area of HRM, the adoption of parent HR policy and practices can either deliberately or unintentionally infuse the culture and strategy of the managing parent firm into the joint venture. Parent control is applied through:

- large numbers and critical placement of parent staff in the joint venture;
- use of parent training facilities in which norms and values of the parent are transferred to JV employees; and
- use of written parent materials (e.g., newsletters) in the joint venture

A further consideration is the level of autonomy versus independence desirable in the joint venture. In instances when the joint venture adopts a large number of policies and practices from the parent firm, the joint venture may inappropriately mirror the parent culture or practices, which may not meet the unique requirements of the venture.

Based on the assignment of management responsibility for the venture, in the early planning stages managers might wish to carefully consider how the division of responsibility between the parents affects the accomplishment of JV strategic objectives. If desirable, planning could include mechanisms for joint parent involvement (especially concerning R&D exchanges through transfers or communication systems) to "legitimize" each parent's contributions.

PART III

Integration of HRM and Strategic Planning

s" on the Library home page)
key financial information on over 15,000 non-US
of the print source: <u>Mergent international news</u>
61 & www.fisonline.com/b/news/b5_news.htm].

s" on the Library home page)
-traded companies. Includes company profiles,
y news summaries, company histories, and

5821)

cks. (HC 106.6 S74)

HF 5549.5 E45 C95 1998
HD 58.8 D344 2001
HD 2746.5 S33 2001
HD 58.8 C3634 1996
HD 2746.5 S34 2000
HD 2746.5 G38 2000
HD 58.5 M36

CHAPTER 6

The Process Experts: A New Role *for* HRM

The key challenges are to facilitate the integration [into the joint venture] of these people coming in from other organizations. To build camaraderie and team spirit. To make sure there is consistency in how people are treated. And I think that as rapidly as possible, to come up with programs in terms of the development and training of employees.

HR Director, Olin

Multiple parent ownership, the presence of diverse national cultures in the same organization, and competitive requirements for fast-paced change present unique and exciting challenges for managers in international joint ventures. For HR managers, in particular, JV complexity creates a demand for a new and intricate role which extends beyond the development of traditional HRM policy and techniques. Consideration must be given to a "process role" to facilitate the integration of people and values within the venture. A process orientation might include, for example, how to assimilate former parent employees into the joint venture, how to deal with changing roles for managers and other employees, or how to create HR policy which is sensitive to the norms and values of employees who represent different national cultures. In international joint ventures, the integration of values and processes is required not only in the joint venture, but between the JV and parent firms as well. These subtle, yet often overlooked features of joint ventures have important implications for both employee satisfaction and corporate success. Although technical HRM competence is a required base condition, a process focus can contribute to greater energy, enthusiasm, and understanding of organizational goals and priorities for employees.

A new, process-oriented role for managers is multifaceted, and demands that managers have personal and political as well as technical skills. Managers will need to act proactively, in concert with other organizational stakeholders. If HRM staff are to be effective in this newly defined and complex role, they require: (1) early involvement, (2) credibility with a wide range of stakeholders, (3) ability and willingness to chart new HR-related values and policy, and (4) adequate staff and financial resources.

A NEW ROLE FOR HR MANAGERS

Fast-paced organizational change necessitates HR managers to readily adapt HR policy to match altered JV strategic priorities. HRM goals and functions are not static in the organization, but are variable and changing. Even in more established ventures such as Mayo Forest Products and Siecor, the companies are in the midst of reorganization plans which necessitate the implementation of major changes to HR policy and process. In order to remain a central player in organizational change, HR managers need flexibility and a willingness to keep pace with strategic revisions in the company as achieved through HRM initiatives.

Related to change in complex organizations like joint ventures, a unique but demanding role for HRM extends beyond traditional HR policy applications in the areas of staffing, reward systems, and performance review, for example. Instead, HRM participation involves the development and implementation of *processes* that foster unity, creativity, and learning. More specifically, a new role for HRM is interactive, based on input from a variety of stakeholders and groups, and focuses on the creation of new value systems and methods. At Diamond Star, HRM staff (as well as other managers and employees) are involved in the creation of a culturally sensitive performance review system. In order to develop HR policy appropriate for both Japanese and American managers, a process was initiated by the HR department to define operating norms of the cultural groups, explain policy rationale, obtain feedback on newly implemented HR policy, and provide training when necessary on the new performance review system. In this way, the development of HR policy involves communication, assessment, and realignment as part of a process orientation for HRM.

A new role for the HR department has several dimensions. HR managers can contribute to the development of:

- *Values*—This implies HR managers know and understand the goals and values of various stakeholders in the parent and JV organizations. A possible role for

HR is the development of the JV mission statement and a vision for the joint venture, in conjunction with others in the venture.

- *Processes*—HR managers might work as the "process experts" to develop and facilitate formal mechanisms for communication (e.g., meetings, a newsletter) and informal communication among subgroups (i.e., between national cultures, union-management groups). Integration will ideally occur both within the joint venture and between the JV and parent companies.

- *Technical HRM Policy*—In a more traditional vein of HR activities, HR managers are responsible for the development of HR policies and practices in the areas of training, reward and recognition, staffing, and performance appraisal.

CHARTING NEW VALUES AND POLICY

An awareness by HR staff of the strategic focus for the joint venture, knowledge of the parent companies, and sensitivity to differences in national and corporate cultures all contribute to the formation of new HR systems which are appropriate for diverse groups. In joint ventures in which employees from the parents and new hires are merged together, operating assumptions and policies that are familiar to employees in the parent firms tend to change. For example, at OCG, new HR policy was created with a goal of integration of former parent employees into the joint venture, in order that they are satisfied with the new policies and environment. At Diamond Star, HR policy was formed based on a consolidation of values and expectations from two diverse cultural groups. In each case, prior to the creation of appropriate policy, HR staff first attempted to define and understand the operating norms and values of the various groups in the venture.

To elaborate, the integration of former parent employees in a newly formed joint venture presents great uncertainty for employees, a situation similar to company mergers. Not only is a physical relocation required for employees, but also an adjustment to new organizational values and processes. Successful adjustment of employees into the venture is more likely to be accomplished when: (1) employees are able to develop a positive identification with the venture, and (2) employee stress is reduced relative to leaving a large multinational firm with which they already identified to join a start-up joint venture about which they know little.

At OCG, where managers expressed a major concern about the integration of a minority group of parent employees to the venture, the integration process was greatly facilitated by emphasis on communication, and the rapid development of new policies with which all employees could identify. This process involves:

- early communication of relevant information to employees about expected changes;

- interviews with employees about their concerns or needs; and
- creation of HR policy that realistically approximates employee expectations (this is especially important in the formation of benefit packages).

Alternately, some HR policies create greater stress for new JV employees, and deserve careful consideration before implementation. These include policies which limit employees from a "bid-back" to the parents for jobs in the near future or a "no choice" assignment to the venture. Although such policies may be instituted with a view to stabilize a newly formed joint venture in the area of staffing, they may be detrimental to committed employee participation in the venture.

BALANCING STAKEHOLDER INTERESTS

Managers are challenged to *balance* the requirements of multiple organizational stakeholders. Different groups within the organization (e.g., union-management, HR-production, Japanese-American) may all have different priorities or operating styles. HR managers gain support from stakeholders by "selling" HR policy prior to its implementation, and by training managers in new HR policy. In these ways, managers and other employees in the joint venture have an opportunity to contribute to the creation of corporate values as reflected in HR policy, and to gain a fuller understanding of the implications of various practices.

In multicultural settings, "stakeholder blessing" of new policies is particularly important; otherwise the implementation of new policy is likely to be subverted or ignored. At Diamond Star, the Japanese Assistant Manager in HR made a special effort to explain HR policy to other Japanese managers, who were otherwise unfamiliar with many of the policies. During the implementation of a new performance appraisal system at Diamond Star, American managers provided information on the system to Japanese managers, asked for implementation feedback, and make assessments related to policy understanding. Japanese managers were not initially comfortable with the performance review process, and training was provided to help the Japanese better understand and operate the system. In this way, values and assumptions of diverse cultural groups were incorporated into new policy, and monitoring was provided by the HR department to determine the effectiveness of policy applications.

Mutual support among diverse groups can be built through frequent formal meetings, and through informal contacts as part of a coalition-building process (Kanter, 1989). As integrators of values and systems, HR managers can organize HR-related processes to provide information exchange across different stakeholders. At OCG, the HR manager created a cross-divisional task team between the R&D and production departments. These two departments had previously viewed their roles and values as separate from one another. The establishment of task groups and cross-training was a conscious move by the HR manager to build greater cooperation and exchange between the units. At Diamond Star, frequent meetings between management and the union resulted in the union's agreement to operate the plant based on a quality-oriented and flexible manufacturing system, which was important to the Japanese partner. In turn, the management at Diamond Star committed to providing job security for employees. Further, related to plant relations between Japanese and American managers, the latter group indicated they were often excluded from vital after-work meetings when important information was shared. Ideally, as part of a process role, members in the HR department would create opportunities (e.g., meetings, training sessions) that formalize the involvement of both groups.

NEW ROLES FOR MANAGERS AND EMPLOYEES

Strategic reorientation complicates the job of HR managers by changing the roles of managers, supervisors, production employees, and union members. In progressive corporations, traditional expectations related to boss-subordinate relationships are gradually being discarded. Instead, new values of how work is to be accomplished prevail, and are focused toward greater involvement by production staff, and the creation of support roles for managers. At Mayo, OCG, Siecor, and Diamond Star, production staff who work in employee involvement systems have been asked by management to accept more responsibility, innovate, and offer improvements to the production process. Consequently, in the creation of new values in the organization, processes are required that facilitate the transition to new roles for both managers and other staff.

For production employees, these changes herald greater participation and perhaps autonomy, although there is skepticism that intended changes in the power or participation structure can be implemented *in practice*. In turn, managers fear a loss of power as many of their responsibilities are shifted to the production floor. These value shifts present opportunities for managers to create a forum in which values and roles can be explored or altered. At Siecor, role shifts were considered in the context of training programs. Both production workers and supervisors receive training in how to work effectively together in teams.

A reorientation of the corporate culture is necessitated on multiple levels—and is central to enhanced corporate competitiveness in firms like joint ventures. As one manager at Siecor suggests, the only way in which the joint venture can meet its operating goals is to "gradually change the culture of the people from one where we've not asked them to use their brains much—to do busy work—to one where they feel they own the business." In turn, some production employees are suspicious that managers will prevent them from accepting newly designated responsibilities. This suspicion was supported by a Diamond Star manager who reported the joint venture had failed to get commitment from some managers to implement the employee involvement systems.

At Mayo Forest Products, Siecor, and Diamond Star, supervisors attempt to retain power through the control of information. Supervisors either do not share information with employees, or they select the content of information which they distribute. A manager at Siecor observes, "empowering people at lower levels in the organization to make decisions traditionally made by them [supervisors] is very threatening, because there's an element of job security that seems to disappear in that." A department head at Siecor advises that in order to give responsibility to production workers, managers need a more "enabling" role. He further explains this is a "radical" step for managers and supervisors.

To counter concerns from production staff that they will actually be allowed greater company involvement, intentions need to be demonstrated in action. To develop employee confidence in a revised culture, hourly workers at Mayo Forest Products are taken to Japan to better observe customer needs and requirements. Employee initiative or suggestions are supported by managers. Some production staff at Siecor are included in supervisory-level meetings, when they were not previously. At Siecor's plants there are no time clocks, and managers say they want to send a deliberate message to employees that they are trusted.

At Mayo Forest Products and Diamond Star, production employees who are part of a union are asked to cooperate with management. At Mayo, cooperation is facilitated through the inclusion of a union representative on the hiring panel for new employees. This step was unique for union-management relations in the mill. At Diamond Star, the relationship with the union was described by managers in the plant as good, and better than in most other automotive assembly plants. The implementation of selected Japanese practices at Diamond Star was aimed at creating "a nonadversarial environment which promotes mutual trust and respect" between managers and union employees.

HRM COORDINATION WITHIN AND ACROSS
ORGANIZATIONAL BOUNDARIES

Within a single organization, a process role for HRM has many dimensions. The role for HRM is even more complicated in international joint ventures, which require not only the creation of appropriate HR systems in the venture, but also the coordination of HRM activities across organizational boundaries. HR managers in joint ventures are required ideally to create processes and systems that link the joint venture and the parents and multiple JV locations, as well as functional units and organizational subgroups within the venture.

HRM systems that inform and link employees both in the joint venture (horizontally and vertically) and between multiple locations (locally and internationally) are important to employee understanding of corporate and, more specifically, HRM initiatives. HRM processes as they operate at Mayo, OCG, Siecor, and Diamond Star are summarized in Table 2. Examples of the kinds of processes that exist at three levels (JV-parent, multiple JV locations, and within the joint venture) are outlined for the joint venture firms.

JV-parent linkages are established through various communication networks and through permanent and temporary employee assignments. Contributions from both parents are encouraged when communication systems are established that link the joint venture and parents. In the area of HR policy formation, HR policies are either adapted from the parent firms, or created uniquely for the venture. In either case, input from multiple sources in the JV and parent firms is desirable. Transfers are another way to coordinate activities across organizational boundaries. In the joint ventures in this study, transfers operate most successfully when employees have a clear understanding of HR policies and the opportunity to express their needs or concerns related to their involvement in the venture. Frequent meetings, orientation programs, and training help reassigned employees to understand new operating conditions, and contribute to commitment and trust-building between members of the JV and parent operations. In ventures where diverse cultures are represented, communication difficulties are overcome through the use of interpreters or "cultural liaisons" who possess bicultural skills.

Coordination among various JV locations occurs through meetings and correspondence. Training in languages, cross-cultural skills, or international management capabilities is an important part of a process to integrate employees and values across different physical locations. Within the joint venture, communication is encouraged across departmental units using task groups or teams, and team training. Vertical integration of managers, supervisors, and production employees is ideally accomplished through open communication, training, and systems that promote mutual involvement of different groups.

In developing a process role for HRM, communication systems, training, and staffing are especially important (refer to Table 2). In some instances, communication was enhanced through training programs. Reconfiguring this information, in Figure 1 JV core requirements and international requirements in the areas of communication, training, and staffing are outlined. Communication systems are open and take many forms, training is broad, and staff are selected who have exemplary personal and technical skills. JV core requirements are important at all levels

TABLE 2
HRM PROCESSES IN INTERNATIONAL JOINT VENTURES

Levels	Processes
1. JV-Parent	
a) management coordination	- facilitation of contributions of both parents (if relevant) through communication networks or job postings in the parent companies - adaptation of HR policy from the parent(s) for the JV, or the creation of new policy for the JV based on input from multiple sources in the JV and in the parents
b) permanently reassigned employees	- solicit feedback on needs and transfer concerns - early establishment and clear communication of HR policy which balances employee security and JV requirements for stability (i.e., carry over of benefits, bid-back to parent policy)
c) temporary transfers	- development of an understanding of the JV environment for transferred employees through orientations and training - creation of conditions of commitment and trust when information is readily shared between the JV and parents - staffing to promote communication across languages and cultures (i.e., interpreters for the transfer of technical expertise; "liaisons" who possess bicultural skills)
2. Multiple JV Locations	
a) locally	- development of mechanisms for information exchange (i.e., meetings, written correspondence)
b) internationally	- facilitation of interpersonal contacts via "world-wide" meetings and teleconferences - training in language skills and cross-cultural skills, and international management skills

TABLE 2 continued

3. Within JV

a) horizontal

- communication across various units (i.e., R&D/manufacturing; HR/production) through cross-team coordination (i.e., <u>cross-departmental teams</u> and <u>task groups</u>) and <u>team training</u>

b) vertical

- creation of <u>open communication</u> between managers, supervisors, and production staff in which there is trust and a willingness to deal with "real issues"; <u>training</u> in role shifts and interpersonal skills
- development of a union-management contract which promotes <u>mutual involvement</u> in activities as well as reciprocal trust and respect

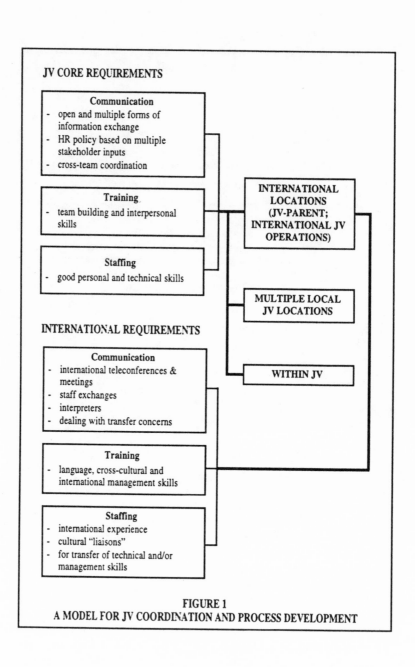

FIGURE 1
A MODEL FOR JV COORDINATION AND PROCESS DEVELOPMENT

of the operation, and international requirements are especially relevant in the JV-parent relationship.

BROAD SKILL REQUIREMENTS

HR staff are most effective as process facilitators if they possess personal, technical, and political skills. JV managers mention the importance of personal skills such as openness and flexibility to new ideas or other perspectives, and tolerance and patience. Technical skills are likewise required. Senior HR managers at OCG, Siecor, and Diamond Star all have many years of experience working in the HR area. In all of the ventures, HR managers have a thorough knowledge of HR policy. Further, HR managers mention that political skills are important for the effective management of relationships with a variety of stakeholders in the JV and parent organizations. More specifically, at Diamond Star, HR managers note the importance of balancing priorities among groups, and the benefits of advance knowledge and information about the groups' concerns and preferences. At OCG, the HR manager recognizes the importance of gaining support from the parents and parent employees assigned to the joint venture in developing new HR policy. The role of HR managers as process experts suggests a revised focus for the HR department in the organization. The HR role will ideally include a knowledge of company strategic goals and objectives in order that HRM policy and practices are in alignment with these goals; the creation and dissemination of a clear vision for HRM at the organizational and HR departmental levels; and an appreciation of how cultural values and assumptions impact employees and the organization.

EARLY HR INVOLVEMENT

Early involvement by HR managers in the JV operation tends to ensure a central and strategic position for HRM in the long term. At OCG, Siecor, and Diamond Star, where the HR departments have a significant role in the creation of HR policy for the venture, the HR staffs were involved in the early stages of planning for the joint venture before the plants were operational. The HR manager at Diamond Star was one of the first staff members hired to the joint venture, and he spent considerable time in Japan determining HR objectives for the joint venture in conjunction with Mitsubishi executives. Along with other staff, the HR manager began to establish HR procedures well in advance of production start-up in the plant. Early involvement by the HR department helps to ensure the HR group is aware of parent strategic initiatives and is able to translate JV objectives into appropriate HRM systems in the venture. On a related note, if the HR department is able to take the lead in effective strategic

HRM planning, and is successful in this task, then quite possibly it will be awarded greater decision-making power as a central player in the future of the company.

When HR policy is established early, then managers in the venture have formalized guidelines to follow for the implementation of various HR practices. This is a special requirement in joint ventures, where former parent staff are relocated to the joint venture and want assurances that benefits and other policies will not be substandard to those enjoyed in the parent company. For instance, at OCG the HR manager immediately began to develop HR policy which she anticipated would be beneficial to employees. Alternately, the early development of some HR policies at Diamond Star was curtailed due to both the large number of policies required, and a need to wait until the union contract was ratified. In the absence of HR policy at Diamond Star, one manager remarks he and others "made up their own policies" as required. In sum, the early establishment of HR policy and guidelines is likely to facilitate a more consistent application of policy in practice.

ESTABLISHING CREDIBILITY

Members of the HR department are viewed as credible when a clearly defined set of HR values and priorities exists with which employees can identify and support. If various HR departmental members are divided as to their role, and which HR values should predominate, then a clear, consistent message as to what is important in the realm of human resources is unlikely to be transmitted to others in the joint venture. One HR manager comments that inconsistency of goals and values within the HR group has, to some extent, resulted in diminished credibility for the department. Within his department, different opinions are expressed as to the amount of employee autonomy and responsibility which should operate in the joint venture. To some degree, the HR department can have a role in the creation of HR-related values in the organization, but this task is compromised until the group can first define a consolidated position for itself.

Although consistency in policy applications is desirable, this does not mean policy should be inflexible and ignore unique situations and requirements. In this sense, the HR mandate is most successful if established policy or rules are balanced with flexibility to meet practical operating considerations. For instance, flexibility and administrative innovation were demonstrated at Diamond Star related to the creation of a new performance appraisal system which was modified significantly from an American version to fit the operating values of both Japanese and American managers in the plant. As another example, at OCG, although a policy was in effect that prohibited employees from bidding back to the parents for two years, this policy could be modified if a transfer back to the parent would clearly be beneficial for employee career development. If the HR department does not introduce flexibility into operating practice, then quite possibly resistance to new operating norms and values will be encountered from JV staff who feel their unique cultural assumptions or operating requirements are overlooked.

Further, support for HR activities by other key players is important in order that HR staff have sufficient power to make policy changes or adjustments. If organizational members feel they have some input to new HR policies, then the job of "selling" policies or strategies to other managers and employees becomes an easier task for HR staff. At OCG and Diamond Star, input from managers and others in the joint venture was requested by the HR department prior to the implementation of policies. This process not only provides the HR department with policy feedback, but serves to build interrelationships and support among various groups in the organization. Alternately, at Mayo Forest Products the HR manager decided to bypass the union committee and provided performance information directly to production employees. The union responded with a flurry of grievances. The HR manager describes this situation in the following way: "We've decided that bypassing the plant committee is not necessarily in our best interests in that they maintain a certain status out in the mill with the crew members. . . . By bypassing them, we do ourselves some harm." In this case, if the HR manager and other managers are to gain organizational support for changes to policies or practices, then first they must secure the approval of key stakeholders in the venture.

RESOURCE REQUIREMENTS

The HR department needs sufficient staff and financial resources to enact a role as "process expert" in the organization. The quality of staff assigned to the HR department should be exemplary—and possess both technical and interpersonal skills if they are to deal with complex HR issues.

OCG and Diamond Star are understaffed in the HR department. Although the HR manager at OCG has a significant role in setting new policy for the venture, she is alone in the department, with administrative assistance. OCG is the only venture in which an HR manager is not located on the production site. Managers and employees in the venture note that locating a member from the HR department in the plant would assist staff in better understanding and consistently applying HR policy and procedure.

At Diamond Star, an HR manager mentions the department would "like to take more of a leadership role, but we've been hampered in doing that from the standpoint that we don't have the number of people to do anything. Right now all we can do is react to things that happen." If the role of HR in the organization is to be proactive in the creation of new HR policy and processes, then sufficient staff are needed for the fulfilment of this mandate.

LESSONS LEARNED

In complex organizations such as international joint ventures, a process role for HRM involves the integration of people and values at multiple levels in the organization. HRM activities are coordinated not only in the venture, but also between the venture and the parent firms. This form of intercompany HR management is rare, and yet has the potential to promote value and policy consistency on a scale which transcends organizational boundaries.

The scope of a process role for HRM is broad—beyond the requirements of traditional HRM policy applications. Subtle process features in joint ventures include a unique HR role which involves, for example: assisting employees to reconfigure their tasks within the venture; integration of minority groups of parent employees into the venture; and interactively creating HR policy in the venture which draws on expertise acquired from diverse parent groups.

A process-oriented role for HRM challenges managers to consider:

- *Values*—clearly define HR values and priorities; understand and balance various stakeholder interests; adapt HR policy and practice in relation to changing organizational needs.
- *Processes*—integrate people and processes through (1) communication systems that are open and operate between and across organizational levels; (2) training to provide skills, information, and values to employees at all levels; and (3) staffing (especially transfers) as a mechanism to create technical or personal linkages between the JV and parent firms.
- *Technical HR Policy*—create HR policy to support the values, strategy, and processes in the venture; develop HR policy early based on multiple sources of input from venture and parent sources.

To effectively traverse this diverse organizational terrain, managers need to be adept negotiators with the necessary resources. More specifically, managers need an awareness of and sensitivity to parent and JV strategy and culture, excellent communication skills, an ability to sell HR policy, as well as technical and political skills. Early HR involvement, and the establishment of credibility among a wide range of stakeholders, will enable a process role to be more readily fulfilled.

CHAPTER 7

Creating an Integrated Whole
of the Venture

What management needs to do is to gain the cohesion and bring the
people together and then develop the sensitivity of programs for the
future. I think when you smash, and this hasn't been a smashing, but
when you integrate organizations I think it's important to, I think, get
people on the same wavelength and make them feel like they're part
of the team, and give a lot of direction.

HR Manager, Olin

An important, yet overlooked area of joint venture relationships is how
diverse groups can be effectively integrated within the venture.[1] How is
unity or trust built? How are employee groups made to feel comfortable
and secure related to their future in the company? What are appropriate
benefits and other HR policies? Of the four joint ventures described here,
OCG represents a good example of the steps that can be taken toward,
and the pitfalls leading to, joint venture integration. The issues related to
JV integration and the role of the HR department are elaborated.

THE MAJOR CHALLENGE: JV INTEGRATION

A majority (90 percent) of the employees allocated to OCG were from
the American parent Olin. The remaining 10 percent were transferred to
OCG from the R&D facility of the Swiss parent that was located in the
United States. Given the major presence of Olin employees in OCG, managers recognized one of the major human resources challenges was the
integration of former Ciba-Geigy staff into the venture. For the group of

employees who were working in Ciba-Geigy's American facility, absorption
into OCG meant a physical relocation and the adoption of new benefits
and other HR policies. As the president of OCG comments, this represents
merging ten percent of the staff who were Ciba-Geigy employees into a
new organization strongly influenced by Olin—an arrangement which creates an "identity crisis" for the minority group of staff.

Although the management at OCG preferred to rapidly transfer Ciba-
Geigy employees to the venture location, a space shortage made this impossible. In this interim period, former Ciba-Geigy (now OCG) employees
remain in the parent offices. One Vice-President remarks, "the problem
is if you keep people at a Ciba-Geigy location, particularly a major one
like a headquarters, they'll relate to the parent company." An important
part of the consolidation process revolves around building a unified corporate culture in the joint venture and forging a new set of organizational
values with which all employees can identify. Much of the responsibility
for integration rests with the HR manager who endeavours to create fair
and consistent policy for all employees. At OCG, HR policy is aimed to
be strategic and aligned to the requirements of the Total Quality Management system. In addition, the HR manager at OCG mentioned the
importance of open lines of communication at all levels of the company.

CONSOLIDATION OF A MINORITY GROUP OF
EMPLOYEES INTO THE JOINT VENTURE

Considerable uncertainty exists for employees who previously have
worked under the protective umbrella of a large multinational corporation, and who now find themselves transferred to a small joint venture
company of approximately 200 people. In the initial stages of the joint
venture, benefit programs and incentive programs were under review, and
it was not clear to employees what their new employment packages would
contain. For some, there was an issue of divided loyalty to the parent firm
and to the joint venture. Employees who were asked to move to another
location had concerns about housing costs and living conditions in the
new area.

Although there are some similarities between the cultures of the parent
firms, there are also differences. Consequently, employees are required to
adjust certain values and procedures in accomplishing their work. Because
OCG is so decentralized, with locations within North America, as well as
separate sites in Europe and Japan, communications matters are complicated.

The management at OCG fully realizes the magnitude of the task of
creating an integrated joint venture from its now separate parts. Integration is to be accomplished on two levels. First is the issue of physical

relocation of people to a new work site. In addition, a looming concern is how to create loyalty to OCG so that employees can enthusiastically identify with the new company and what it has to offer.

CHOOSING A PARTNER WITH A SIMILAR CORPORATE CULTURE

Although there are no crystallized solutions for creating integration in a joint venture, one Vice-President at Ciba-Geigy mentions the importance of choosing a partner with a relatively similar corporate culture. To an extent, parent culture similarity reduces the degree to which employees must readjust values and norms. In addition, if HR policy and structures can be created early in the JV life-cycle, then employees have more information about and less uncertainty regarding benefits and entitlements, or managerial expectations. The Ciba-Geigy Vice-President elaborates,

I think the more things you can resolve before the first official day that people cohabitate as one business, the better off you're going to be. Because what you find out if you don't do that, it's kind of play as you go and you have people in this extraordinary position in that on one hand they know they are part of this new venture, but on the other hand they're being treated as they were always treated when they were part of your venture. And I think there's probably some internal schizophrenia that's going on trying to figure out how to behave and what to do and what to respond to.

Various employees note that differences between the two parent cultures relate to size, and to some extent to the national origin of the parents. Olin is smaller, more entrepreneurial, with a tradition of informality. In contrast, a Ciba-Geigy executive observes the European company is more bureaucratic and conservative than most American companies. He adds "the Europeans are much more conservative in their approach to decision making . . . we tend to be perhaps a little more forgiving around results because of our preoccupation with the longer term . . . we tend to be a little more paternalized."

DEVELOPMENT OF HR POLICY

In order to forge an HR policy which was strategically and culturally appropriate for the joint venture, the HR manager at OCG actively solicited the opinions of managers and other employees of both parent companies. Both the Director of Human Resources for Electronic Materials at Olin and the Vice-President of Human Resources for Ciba-Geigy U.S. were involved in the developmental stages of HR planning at OCG. Initial discussions were primarily centered on the transfer and integration of employees to OCG, and the development of benefit and compensation systems. The senior HR managers from each of the parent firms continue to be associated with OCG's HR manager in the creation of various policies for the venture.

In the initiation of new HR policy for OCG, the HR manager in the venture notes that the HR objectives and policies of the parent companies are very similar. The policies of both parents are considered and then one policy is chosen over another, or policy is created unique to OCG. The venture's HR manager remarks most guidance comes from Olin. For example, the venture HR manager receives assistance from the labor department of Olin on issues related to OCG hourly employees. The Vice-President of HR for Ciba-Geigy United States was involved in the review of a new benefits package.

ASSESSMENT OF EMPLOYEE REQUIREMENTS

To determine employee attitudes and needs, the HR manager at OCG interviewed many of the employees who were designated to become part of the venture. The HR manager visited with former Ciba-Geigy employees for one day every two weeks to provide information about the joint venture and to answer questions. To reduce anxiety about the move, a "Family Night" was planned for new JV employees and their spouses. The intent of the evening was to present information on the relocation area and to highlight policy provisions. A relocation task force was created to consider how best to phase the transfer of people to the joint venture.

Beyond specific relocation concerns, OCG managers focus on communication as important to the realization of personal goals, as well as to the strategic requirements of the venture. OCG has numerous mechanisms in place to facilitate communication among its various branches. For example, members of the headquarters office routinely travel to the JV production facility to participate in meetings. Task teams are used extensively and operate as one vehicle to obtain employee input from multiple sources and locations. Task groups have been assembled to consider a variety of issues, including quality, recognition, environmental issues, and benefits programs. There is a company newsletter.

EARLY INCONSISTENCIES IN HR POLICY

Early in the JV start-up, the HR manager aimed to develop HR policy which could be applied consistently to all employees. In the areas of nonmonetary recognition or training, program consistency was quickly established. However, in other areas such as pay and benefits, the implementation of consistent HR programming was difficult because former Ciba-Geigy employees designated to OCG were to remain under the policy umbrella of the Swiss parent until a formal move to the joint venture was possible. Related to this arrangement, employees who relocated from Ciba-Geigy into OCG would do so under the Ciba-Geigy relocation policy. Even after the JV start-up, former Ciba-Geigy employees initially continued to operate under that parent's policies for tuition reimbursements and vacation entitlements. Alternately, employees who were transferred to the joint venture from Olin continued to operate under the policies of the American parent. In this respect both Ciba-Geigy and Olin employees who initially transferred to OCG functioned under separate benefit systems.

In addition, a unique feature of OCG during the first year was the leasing of Ciba-Geigy employees to the venture. This group of employees remained on Ciba-Geigy's payroll system and the expense to the parent company was billed back to OCG. Once the former Ciba-Geigy group physically relocated into the joint venture, they were integrated into the OCG compensation policy and payroll system. Former Olin employees transferred permanently to OCG were not leased, and instead fell under the JV compensation system. This policy discrepancy between the two groups resulted from United States regulatory characteristics and was implemented as an interim step to avoid a multi-employer pension plan. As a result, separate compensation systems existed for former Olin and Ciba-Geigy (now all OCG) employees during the early stages of the venture.

THE STAFFING DILEMMA

Managers at OCG and at the parent companies attempted to assemble HR policies that best suited venture employees. However, in some instances requirements for a quick and efficient start-up were incompatible with employee preferences or concerns. For example, to some extent employees had no other option than to join OCG. Exact entitlements and time frames for the move into the joint venture were not initially known, exacerbating employee anxiety. Finally, in order for the joint venture to stabilize, managers thought it critical for R&D staff to remain in the joint venture without being able to bid back to the parent company for a period of two years. One Vice-President at Ciba-Geigy summarizes some of the staffing issues related to the transfer of the minority group of Ciba-Geigy employees to the joint venture in the following way:

Let me start first by saying I think they [former Ciba-Geigy employees] were angry . . . they had no option. This is quite unlike we're going to sell the company and they want you to come to work for them. Do you want to and if not we have a job for you elsewhere. When you form a joint venture and you're going to have a 50 percent piece of it, one of the things you find out very early in the game is you're not going to give key players very many options. I mean you're certainly not going to try to keep them within Ciba-Geigy to the detriment of your new 50/50 interest. . . . So consequently, you give them no lifelines whatsoever and what you say to them in effect, the proposition to the Ciba-Geigy group was: (1) The only job you have available is to go to work for OCG; (2) It happened so quickly we have not sorted out every little detail around your benefit entitlements but suffice it to say that they'll be comparable; (3) We know your circumstance is uncertain and you don't know your new boss and so forth and so on, but trust us it will be O.K. We have no idea what their culture is but we think it is similar to ours; (4) We know that longer term we'd like to consolidate the Ciba-Geigy group into the joint venture. We have an idea what time frame that may be. We're not positive every one of you here will have a job, but we think most of you would be offered the opportunity. And oh, by the way, we know most of you have never relocated before so we accept the fact there is a lot of uncertainty associated with that circumstance; and (5) would be the issue of while you're there and doing the job for OCG don't bother to bid for other jobs within the Ciba-Geigy Corporation because we're not accepting your bid. Now the corollary to that is we'll provide things like a stick-around bonus and an incentive to stay to the end. And a promise that you'll be treated reasonably and that if you make a certain date, we'll let you bid on anything within Ciba-Geigy, which is in two years.

The no bid back to jobs in the parent companies for a period of two years applies to Olin as well as Ciba-Geigy employees. The policy was initiated when some employees bid for lateral or lesser positions inside Ciba-Geigy to avoid joining OCG. In certain circumstances, exceptions to the no bid policy can be made. An Olin executive explains,

This restriction doesn't preclude someone being able to transfer if OCG management no longer needs a particular skill, and the parent is willing or has a position for that person back with the parent. There should be nothing to keep that from happening. What you do need to put a block in though is the matter of choice where the employee chooses to move, creating a hole which jeopardizes the joint venture.

Further, employees may transfer from OCG back to the parent company if the move is promotional and enhances career development. The two-year no-bid policy is supported by both parent companies, and applies to European as well as North American operations.

A concern over relocation also existed for OCG employees in Switzerland. Of 20 to 25 Ciba-Geigy employees in Switzerland, three were to become OCG employees and the others were to be leased to the joint venture. As the Vice-President of Finance and Administration at OCG clarifies,

The issue with the three people, it's been a difficult issue getting them to become OCG employees because they had concerns about whether they would be forced to relocate out of Switzerland. They wanted some guarantees that they would not be relocated. We're not going to give them that guarantee because even Ciba-

Geigy wouldn't give them that guarantee. And they wanted sort of a parachute to go back to Ciba-Geigy under certain conditions. And the only two conditions that will permit that is that if they are fired from OCG, Ciba-Geigy will take them back or if the Ciba-Geigy ownership of 50 percent of OCG is changed, then Ciba-Geigy would take them back. So it's been like pulling teeth, apparently, just to get those three people and to have a suitable negotiated contract.

FORGING A JOINT VENTURE UNITY

In the context of the newly formed venture, several management challenges exist. According to the HR manager, employee concerns (particularly those of former Ciba-Geigy employees) need to be addressed by the venture management team in order to gain employee commitment to OCG. More specifically, two of the main issues for consideration are:

- how to deal with employee apprehension related to policy inconsistency (e.g., pay and benefits), and whether HR policy is considered by employees to be "fair"; and

- how to develop a feeling of loyalty by employees to the joint venture, particularly given the initial period when employees were leased from the parent and had no option other than to join the venture, and were generally not permitted to bid for jobs in the parent for a period of two years.

In order to address these areas, HR managers from the parent firms have worked with the OCG HR manager to create new human resources policy. Input to this process has been solicited from various groups of OCG employees. The HR manager for OCG indicated to staff members that their needs in the venture were to be considered and accommodated whenever possible. During the first two years of JV operation, HR policy in the areas of pay and benefits was expected to operate on a consistent basis for all employees. However, whether employees would perceive salary or benefit policies as being fair in relation to what they had previously received from the parent was uncertain.

However, the more complex issue for managers is how to create a value system unique to OCG that employees might embrace, and through which they may ultimately form affiliations and loyalties to the venture as opposed to the parent firms. To achieve this goal, company values are communicated to employees through presentations about OCG's strategic orientation. Occasionally, the President of OCG addresses employees to discuss the progress of the new venture. In addition, employees have the opportunity to meet with managers in small groups and ask questions related to OCG operations. For example, "quality luncheons" are hosted by OCG management for groups of ten to twelve employees who are drawn randomly from multiple levels in the organization. The purpose of the luncheons is to share information about the company with employees, and to encourage company participation. Further, company dinners are arranged to recognize employee performance and to communicate to employees what is valued behavior in the company.

ISSUES PROBLEMATIC TO JV INTEGRATION

One of the strengths of OCG is its presence on three continents. In the fast-moving semiconductor industry this permits OCG to develop and manufacture products to meet specific customer demands, and to provide prompt supply, delivery, and technical support to markets in Europe, North America, and the Pacific Rim.

However, at the same time the decentralized nature of the company makes the development of a consistent, united corporate culture elusive. In the United States there are multiple OCG locations, and the executive staff, including the JV President, Vice-Presidents, and HR Manager, are in a different location from the manufacturing facility. Most managers express that eventually they would prefer to see senior OCG managers on the operations site. A Director suggests having employees in one location is "how you really build unified culture." Although modern communication like telephone and fax are adequate, he continues, "there is no substitute for face-to-face communication."

Employees are provided with information about the company in the employee handbook and newsletter. In each case, the information distributed to OCG staff is originally produced for Olin and describes that parent's philosophies and benefits, as opposed to the strategies and philosophies specific to OCG. Some managers questioned whether a newsletter and handbook that focus primarily on the American parent allow OCG to develop an identity as a separate company.

Finally, training is provided to OCG employees at the Olin training facility. Although there are definite cost advantages in using established training programs and staff from the parent, at the same time one might question how former Ciba-Geigy employees feel about this arrangement. In this context, the former Ciba-Geigy group might possibly view their training as preparation for participation in an Olin subsidiary operation, rather than for involvement in a 50/50 joint venture company.

LESSONS LEARNED

Managers in newly formed joint ventures typically focus attention on technological, financial, or marketing issues. Less often is significant attention paid to the operation of strategic human resource management practices related to the integration of parent employees into the venture. At OCG, where one parent supplies the majority of JV staff, issues may arise for the minority group related to future entitlements; to a requirement to relocate; or to divided loyalty between the multinational parent to which they formerly belonged and the neophyte joint venture about which relatively little is known.

At OCG considerable attention was focused on the development and implementation of appropriate HR policy and practice. Integration of parent employees to the joint venture is achieved in two ways: (1) creation of technical HR policy (e.g., benefit entitlements) and (2) development of values with which employees can identify as part of the corporate culture of OCG. More specifically, the process of integration involves:

1. Early, consistent implementation of "fair" HR policy.
2. Establishment of open lines of communication within the joint venture and between the joint venture and parents.
   - involvement of HR professionals from both parents in HR policy formation
   - input from the minority group of parent employees who are merged into OCG
3. Overcoming problems related to employees who feel greater loyalty to the parent than to the joint venture.
   - employee insecurity pertaining to leaving the parent multinational to join a start-up joint venture
   - HR policies that inadvertently magnify employee concerns
4. Forging a new set of values unique to the joint venture as opposed to the adoption of parent values.
   - issues relate to training, mechanisms for sharing company information (e.g. newsletters, handbooks)
5. Other:
   - information on employee requirements in the joint venture is actively solicited (e.g., establishment of a relocation task force)
   - information on changes is provided (e.g., employment packages, manager's expectations)
   - transfer of former parent employees to the joint venture is completed as swiftly as possible
   - open lines of communication are developed (e.g., meetings, task teams, a JV company newsletter)
   - training is provided to enhance JV-specific goals and identity.

NOTE

1. Excerpts in this chapter are adapted with permission from Dianne J. Cyr, "OCG Microelectronic Materials," in J. Roos (ed.), *European Casebook on Cooperative Strategies* (New York: Prentice-Hall, 1994).

CHAPTER 8

Communication Systems to Enhance Integration and Learning

You have your technical business meetings going on between us and them [the parents] all the time. The linkages run all throughout the company from the lowest level to the highest level. ... With geography, with 4,000 miles apart where the parents are located, two different cultures, a couple of languages to throw around, communications do take a lot of traveling, and a lot of precision.

Executive, Siecor

Communication is especially important in joint ventures, where information needs to keep flowing not only within a single company, but between the joint venture and parents, and between international locations of the venture as well. Communication systems which are open, and which operate both horizontally and vertically in the venture, contribute to the degree employees know about JV goals and objectives, and about management's intentions regarding products, processes, and policies.

In joint ventures involving multiple cultural groups, communication presents special challenges. At Diamond Star, managers and other employees note communication difficulties are the most serious problem in the plant. Across cultures, information exchange is enhanced by the use of illustrations and interpreters, and through an understanding of the cultural norms for communication of different cultural groups.

Although technical sharing of information between the joint venture and parents is important for product development and technological learning, communication may be hampered by product "secrecy," or when the recipient of the information is considered an "outsider." Building organizational trust and commitment are important prerequisites for information exchange between groups.

MULTIPLE FORMS OF COMMUNICATION

A strong emphasis on communication needs to occur within the joint venture, as well as in the creation of intercompany linkages between the JV and parent firms. A large number and variety of communication systems exist at Mayo Forest Products, OCG, Siecor, and Diamond Star. The upper management group in each joint venture has a commitment to share information with other managers and employees, and as a result many formal channels for information exchange operate. Mayo Forest Products, the smallest joint venture in the study, probably has the most intensive communication systems, in order to provide all levels of staff with information on a consistent basis. OCG, with operations on three continents, has special requirements related to the creation of integrated communication networks. Mechanisms for information exchange at OCG are in place, not only within individual locations, but also between the North American, European, and Japanese locations. With various sites in the United States, Siecor is challenged to integrate communication systems between the separate plant and branch locations of the joint venture. Siecor has also set up a special communication network with Siemens related to the sharing of product information. Diamond Star has multiple forms of communication but as managers and other employees in the venture note, there have been ongoing difficulties with information exchange systems. In part, this is related to the presence of two distinct cultures and languages in the plant. The forms of communication which operate in each joint venture are summarized in Figure 2.

An overview of the communications mechanisms present in these four joint ventures reveals a primary emphasis on face-to-face meetings. In most of the joint ventures, meetings are scheduled on a regular basis. This includes meetings related to: JV boards, the JV advisory committee, daily production, maintenance, departments, crews, safety, quality and continuous improvement teams, task teams, executive planning, focus groups, Quality Circles, Kaizen, and, in the case of OCG, "world-wide" meetings. The exchange of technical information occurs between members (especially in R&D) of the parent companies and the joint venture. The active sharing of information is viewed by most managers as central to their operations. In addition to meetings, information is exchanged among personnel through the use of fact sheets, memos, bulletin boards and suggestion boxes. Some form of company newsletter and an employee handbook are available to staff in all of the joint ventures. The two largest joint ventures, Diamond Star and Siecor, have closed-circuit television. In all of the joint ventures there is extensive use of the telephone. At OCG,

MAYO FOREST PRODUCTS	SIECOR
fact sheets bulletin boards company newsletter handbook meetings: daily production daily maintenance dept. managers (weekly) superintendent (weekly) crew (weekly) safety quality improvement teams (QIT) continuous improvement (CIT)	memos bulletin boards closed circuit T.V. voice mail newsletter headquarters meetings: executives (weekly) senior managers (monthly) communication Koffee Klatches plant meetings: focus groups daily production pre-shift (weekly) quality QIT, CAT, CIT management/R&D
OCG	DIAMOND STAR
bulletin boards suggestion box memos task teams Quality lunches research reports meetings handbook newsletter international teleconferences world-wide meetings	white boards newsletter bulletin boards Quality Circle (QC) News closed circuit T.V. meetings: informal (Japanese) QC/Kaizen production supervisory (daily) departmental

FIGURE 2
COMMUNICATION SYSTEMS AT MAYO, OCG, SIECOR, AND DIAMOND STAR

every two weeks international teleconferences are held to link managers across three continents. Unique to Siecor, much importance is attached to a voice mail system (for both managers and the experimental work teams in Plant 1) as a way of exchanging information among busy managers, or across shifts. Diamond Star facilitates communication across multiple languages by using slides and visual aids (e.g., white boards).

COMMUNICATION THROUGH OPEN SYSTEMS

The most successful communication systems are open and operate horizontally and vertically to inform employees about JV goals and objectives. Turning first to an examination of horizontal communication, information is frequently exchanged between multiple hierarchical levels (e.g., between managers, supervisors, and production staff). For example at Mayo Forest Products, generally staff at all levels felt they had a good knowledge of the business, and of management's intentions. Production employees at Mayo said they receive information through weekly meetings and from bulletin boards. Performance data for the mill are available from fact sheets posted on bulletin boards every morning. The monthly company newsletter provides departmental summaries on performance, quality and production updates, marketing information, and safety statistics. Each morning during a production meeting, managers and supervisors share information on mill activities for the 24-hour period. Managers, superintendents, and mill crews each have weekly information meetings. In the crew meetings, actual performance is compared to goals the group has set for itself. In addition, meetings are held as required to inform employees of capital improvements, product development, equipment changes, and training programs. As one employee at Mayo comments, "everybody can see where we stand." Although some supervisors did withhold information from employees, generally production staff noted they are well informed. Managers at Mayo Forest Products said there are "no secrets."

Quality luncheons at OCG are hosted by managers for small groups of employees in order to exchange ideas. The President of OCG addresses employees on an occasional basis to discuss JV progress. In the OCG manufacturing facility, employees receive information through weekly production meetings and memos; supervisors meet together each morning to discuss daily progress. There is an employee suggestion box, and bulletin boards display job postings, safety information, and social events. Employees are encouraged to express their ideas to management, and the production manager notes he has "an open door policy and people can speak up and say what they want."

At the corporate office, communication among executives at Siecor is facilitated through weekly meetings during which the President and Vice-

Presidents of the company meet to discuss major issues and directions for the venture. Other upper-level managers meet on a monthly basis. As one executive notes, "Communication is very good at the middle and upper management level because we have business teams that meet every month and discuss the business at a very high level, and discuss outside forces and things that are going on that influence the business." The outcomes of the monthly meetings are passed to lower level managers through both written communications and informal channels.

Monthly and quarterly communication meetings for Siecor employees are organized through an internal communications supervisor in the personnel department. The content of the meetings includes the financial performance of Siecor over the previous month, new products, safety, and other issues. Guest speakers discuss markets, ongoing projects, success stories, and failures. In Siecor's plants, regular meetings are held for managers and production employees. Quality meetings focus specifically on the production of quality products, and minutes from meetings of Corrective Action Teams and Continuous Improvement Teams are posted on a bulletin board.

A production worker at Siecor remarks that shift supervisors "are wonderful to keep us informed on administrative type things, manufacturing changes . . . they're great about communication." At the headquarters office and in the plants, focus groups provide employees with a face-to-face chance to ask questions of managers related to any aspect of the company. Management's challenge is to establish a norm of trust and sharing for the meetings. As the sessions operated, some production staff were hesitant to discuss "real issues" for fear of appearing uncooperative.

In addition to vertical systems of communication and coordination, horizontal communication *across levels* (i.e., between various units and employee teams) is considered important. At Siecor, cross-team coordination is accomplished by a team project manager for production, who arranges weekly meetings for coordinators on each shift. These meetings are established to facilitate the integration and coordination of efforts and communication across teams. At OCG, cross-functional teams and task forces likewise create communication links across organizational units. To coordinate OCG's various international operations, business managers representing Europe, the United States, and Japan attend "world-wide" meetings. Participants review JV progress, look at the competitive market situation, and consider future plans for OCG. Further, at Mayo, Siecor, and Diamond Star, a newsletter which focuses on the joint venture, rather than on more general parent operations, helps to draw JV personnel together as a unit.

In general, active forms of communication that involve the direct interaction of employees in the joint ventures are more favored by employees than passive forms of information exchange such as memos, reports, or newsletters. One manager observes that although telephone and fax are adequate, "there is no substitute for face-to-face communication." Several managers mentioned the importance of establishing personal contacts with their counterparts, in meetings involving face-to-face interactions. A manager at Siecor notes that the development of personal relationships significantly enhanced his ability to discuss future issues with his contacts by telephone. The temporary assignment of personnel from the parents to the venture provides an opportunity for managers or other staff to work together over a period of time, and to gain a better understanding of one another.

CONSTRAINTS TO INFORMATION EXCHANGE

Communication systems operate with relative efficiency at Mayo Forest Products, OCG, and Siecor. In contrast, at Diamond Star, staff at various levels indicated there had been ongoing difficulties in this area. Multiple languages spoken in the Diamond Star plant contribute to information exchange problems. However, apart from culturally-related factors, other conditions have made information exchange problematic. For instance, some supervisors "hoarded" information to retain power. Differences in departmental goals or priorities sometimes resulted in selective distribution of information within one's own group. In order to allow information to flow more freely, top-down decisions are needed to support information sharing as a company norm in the joint venture. Of importance, the forms of information exchange used (e.g., memos, meetings at the production level) must be implemented in practice.

To elaborate, the initial intent at Diamond Star was to create an open style of communication, with maximal information passed between managers and other employees in order to facilitate employee involvement in the operation of the company. As at Mayo Forest Products, OCG, and Siecor, numerous communication systems operate at Diamond Star. The monthly company newsletter informs staff about quality circles, department roles and activities, community events, car model changes, awards given to vehicles produced at Diamond Star, production/sales statistics, contributions the company makes to the community, and a list of those people who received promotions. Meetings are held at multiple levels in the plant in order to advise employees of new developments. Employees convene their own meetings related to quality circle and Kaizen processes. On occasion the President of Diamond Star is seen walking in the plant talking to production staff. In office areas, an absence of walls allows employees easy access to one another.

Despite the variety of mechanisms for formal communication, one Diamond Star manager mentions that in day-to-day operations open communication and employee participation has not been accomplished.

Another manager remarks that part of the communication breakdown occurs because some group leaders are not receiving information from upper level managers, in order to then pass it to production workers. A production employee concurs that "communication is a big factor. I've talked to several of my supervisors about it. It [information] just doesn't filter down. There's too much secrecy imposed. . . . Usually when we want to know something we go to manufacturing." He continues that in some cases, even when the group leader does obtain information, he will choose to withhold it from the group members. This worker further volunteered that he thought it would be useful to have memos sent to each production group from management for posting on a bulletin board which everyone can read. Although some group leaders do not provide updates to employees, others do. One group leader remarks that every day at the beginning of a shift he conducts a short meeting during which he tells associates about production levels for the previous day, production expectations for the shift, and other, miscellaneous news.

At the upper management level, managers have mixed reactions as to how communication systems operate. Some managers feel that because of communication difficulties, it is "impossible to get the job done at all." Other managers mention they are satisfied with the amount of information provided, and in turn share it with the managers who report to them. An HR manager believes a "top-down decision" is required that commits Diamond Star to greater information sharing, and to the establishment of superior mechanisms for the distribution of information. Further, he mentions it would be advantageous if manufacturing would better inform the HR group of content to be passed to the floor, so HR could put this information into a format for distribution.

COMMUNICATION BARRIERS DUE TO LANGUAGE

In joint ventures where a significant number of managers and other staff are from different national cultures, communication systems are likely to be complicated by multiple languages, and diverse cultural norms and values. Employees at Diamond Star said communication was probably the biggest problem in the plant. Although many of the Japanese at Diamond Star speak English, subtle differences in communication styles often resulted in frustration or miscommunication. Language barriers are bridged by using illustrations, interpreters, and "cultural liaisons" with bicultural skills.

One Japanese Vice-President at Diamond Star remarks that when differences in opinion occur between Japanese and American managers they are often "based on misunderstanding or lack of proper communications." He mentions the lack of English language skills as a problem, and that often "both sides get frustrated. . . . Basically I think we [the Japanese] are trying, trying to understand, or trying to explain. It's a long process in any joint venture." A manager remarks it is interesting that Americans come into Diamond Star with the full knowledge the company has a different culture and language differences, and yet they show little patience in communication with Japanese colleagues.

Beyond the physical competence required to speak a language, the ability to effectively communicate between cultural groups is embedded in an individual's desire to take the time and effort to initiate information exchanges. An appreciation of different communication styles is imperative. One manager who is equally skilled in both American and Japanese language and culture remarks,

Flexibility is very important, and the tolerance of ambiguity. Now ambiguity is something that stems from the Japanese language and culture. And the Japanese will never come out and say things very straightforwardly. The Japanese will go round and round the bush in ten different ways . . . but what he's telling you is I don't like that idea, it's not acceptable.

In contrast, a Japanese manager remarks, "American people are very much outspoken and sometimes upset some Japanese because they are so straight or so outspoken."

At Diamond Star, the inability by Americans and Japanese to understand one another's language partially is bridged by the use of interpreters and illustrations. Interpreters are predominantly used on the plant floor to help Japanese technical assistants and coordinators (who are providing manufacturing expertise) communicate with American managers and production workers. Illustrations are also helpful, and both Japanese and Americans write down content and diagrams on a white board. An American manager remarks, "We did a lot of illustrating through sketches and this was very helpful to overcome this language barrier." In other written communication, another American manager notes the Japanese prefer to see graphs and charts.

The exchange of technical information was less problematic than other areas of communication. One Japanese executive at Diamond Star considers technical exchanges to be "very successful," resulting from a common technical language shared by Japanese and American engineers in the plant. This finding is given support by Lewis (1990: 258), who suggested that around the world, scientists and engineers in the same discipline are,

Educated with the same principles, use the same texts, read the same journals, and share the same jargon. . . . Thus, more than any other discipline, science and technology share many values that cut across other cultural boundaries.

Further, a Japanese employee at OCG who considers himself a "liaison" between various groups in the venture assists with the translation of reports—trying to capture the underlying meaning and intent of the Japanese text. At Diamond Star, the two managers with bicultural skills fill a similar role.

Alternately, few Americans have multiple language or cultural skills. A Japanese manager at Diamond Star remarks, "there is much hesitancy on the part of Americans to learn a foreign language. Generally, Americans expected members of the other culture to speak English." At Siecor, one manager notes the German staff with whom he communicates were all conversant in English. American managers at Siecor remark that the ability on the part of the Germans to speak English had greatly enhanced the communication process in the venture.

INFORMAL OPERATING NORMS

Communication is influenced not only by multiple languages, but by the existence of different informal norms for information exchange related to national culture. Although the American and the Japanese cultural groups have differing communication norms, the norms operating in the Japanese group have the greatest impact. In large part this is because the Japanese parent has manufacturing and management responsibility for Diamond Star, and in this role provides strategic information to the plant through Japanese managers on assignment from the parent company. To overcome communication barriers between groups due to different operating norms, HRM staff can help to institutionalize meetings that involve all relevant parties.

Partly due to language ease, and partly due to familiarity, Japanese managers at Diamond Star meet in informal groups after work to exchange information. This form of interaction has the automatic effect of excluding American managers and possibly preventing them from obtaining strategic or other technical information which Japanese managers might possess. Some of the American managers at Diamond Star view this segregation with concern, and feel "left out" of the mainstream of information exchange. A manager in manufacturing at Diamond Star notes his Japanese counterparts have information before it reaches him. He remarks,

The communication, for example, in terms of tasks . . . seems to come down through the Mitsubishi side, and everyone on the Mitsubishi side, including our TAs [technical assistants] and coordinators . . . they seem to know what's going on. At all levels information filters through the Japanese ranks. Then we have official meetings to explain, to disseminate the information, to assign the responsibilities, or whatever. And what's always the case is that all the Japanese people are already dialed in.

With respect to HR matters, in some instances Japanese managers directly interact with the Vice-President of HRM (who is a representative of Mitsubishi), rather than deal directly with the American HR manager with relevant functional responsibility. In other divisions, American managers report that a Japanese manager may consult with a Japanese coordinator, and bypass the branch manager in charge of a project. With reference to these examples, important information in the joint venture often is passed through informal, nondesignated information channels rather than through a more formal and institutionalized information system. Individuals who are "outsiders" are not privy to all levels of company information, and this affects an employee's ability to accomplish tasks, and the degree of job satisfaction which they experience.

Informal communication systems also exist at Mayo, OCG, and Siecor— but less powerfully than the informal systems at Diamond Star. In shared management joint ventures between partners from widely diverse national cultures, one might expect informal communication systems to be more prevalent than in companies made up of culturally similar groups. Such reliance on informal systems may result from members of different national cultures gravitating toward operating styles and norms and group interactions which are the most familiar.

SHARING TECHNICAL INFORMATION

In international joint ventures, especially when the goal of the parents is to create value-added products, technology sharing from the parents to the venture is necessary. However, information exchange among the JV-parent groups is complicated when individuals feel that providing sensitive information compromises the parent's strategic position (related to, for example, product secrecy or innovative technology). Ideally, open exchange of technical information will occur when a climate of trust is established through staff transfers, key placement of R&D staff, and joint meetings between parent and JV personnel. Before information can be exchanged, a variety of pitfalls must first be overcome.

To elaborate, one might expect more open exchanges of information between parent employees in the headquarters office and that same parent's staff who are transferred to the venture. In each case, they are "insiders" and belong to one parent organization. Staff who are transferred to the joint venture from the parent firm are still considered members of the parent, and therefore they are more likely to receive privileged information. This is in contrast to "cross-parent" information sharing. To some extent, managers or technical staff from one parent may be reluctant to share information with staff from the other parent, even though they all contribute to the benefit of the venture firm.

In support of this supposition, a Siemens employee on assignment to the R&D division at Siecor remarks he is more likely than an "outside" employee (either from Siecor or from the American parent Corning) to have access to information from the German parent company and its subsidiaries. Alternately, an engineer from Siemens mentions that he had experienced difficulty trying to obtain technical information from Corning. In this sense, the extent to which members of the JV and parent firms either screen or share information has implications for the amount of technical learning possible in the venture. If managers of the parent firms commit to a joint venture in which the aim is to create value-added products (as was the case in Siecor), then at the most senior levels of the venture, mechanisms and norms should be established which support open information exchange as it affects the joint venture.

At Siecor, the placement of a Siemens employee in the position of Vice-President of Cable Technology has significantly contributed to information transfer from Siemens to the venture. Further, information exchange can be enhanced if rewards for managers and other employees are based on *joint* product development (although this did not appear to happen in the joint ventures in this investigation). If norms for openness and collaboration do not exist, information may be restricted between the parents and joint venture, which in the long term may affect the ability of managers to realize technical, as well as interpersonal, opportunities in the venture. Employees who feel they are unable to accomplish tasks due to a constricted flow of information may eventually feel demoralized, and question their continued participation in the venture.

Although in general one might expect to see more frequent and open exchanges between headquarters' and other employees who belong to the same parent firm, there are some conditions which moderate how these communications operate. For instance, at Diamond Star, some of the Chrysler task force (those who remained in the venture and who were committed to the JV goals) began to feel more a part of the venture than the parent. In fact, as one Chrysler manager observes, he has a more valued role at Diamond Star than in the parent organization. Specifically, he remarks, "We made an earnest effort to help and got involved [at Diamond Star]. And those of us who did are appreciated more than we ever could have been back home [at Chrysler] because we helped fill some of those cultural gaps." This Chrysler manager expresses an allegiance to the venture, and a desire to focus his energies to help Diamond Star succeed. As loyalty by parent employees to the joint venture increases, and if there is minimal appreciation of efforts by the parent firm, a gradual reduction in the amount of information exchanged between the relocated parent employee and his or her counterparts at the headquarters office might be expected. At Diamond Star, this has implications for the accomplishment of parent goals. Originally, Chrysler entered the venture to learn from the Japanese partner, and sent Chrysler employees to Diamond Star for this purpose. As Chrysler transferees either returned to the parent, or gradually reduced parent ties, then the accomplishment of this goal was reduced.

Related to the exchange of technical information in the human resources department, at Siecor senior HR managers attend HR meetings coordinated by Corning. The purpose of the meetings is to exchange information about HR activities in the various Corning organizations. There is also an annual HR conference organized by Corning which is available to a wider range of human resources staff. Apart from these formalized meetings, the HR managers at Siecor are in frequent (usually weekly) contact with their counterparts at Corning. Although there are no formal meetings between the personnel groups at Siecor and Siemens, the Manager of Employee Relations at Siecor mentions there are two or three people in the HR function at Siemens with whom they share information and arrange transfers. Communication between HR staff in the venture and parent organizations facilitated the formation of valuable contacts through which strategic and, more specifically, HR-related information was exchanged.

LESSONS LEARNED

Although the activation and monitoring of communication systems is not traditionally considered a role of the HR department, there is evidence to suggest that HR staff can play a meaningful part in linking various groups in the joint venture and between the JV and parent firms. The most successful communication systems are multifaceted and form connections between groups both horizontally and vertically—with special emphasis on pushing information down to the production level of the organization. Open norms for communication must be demonstrated in practice if employees are to risk the discussion of "real issues" of concern. As in other forms of organizations beside joint ventures, active forms of communication are considered most desirable.

Culture differences and language present special barriers to communication that can be bridged by interpreters or cultural liaisons. When different cultural operating norms are present, the HR group can assist in the institutionalization of meetings involving relevant parties in order that the non-dominant cultural group doesn't feel left out of the decision-making processes.

CHAPTER 9

Staffing to Win

When we go to hire staff here we don't ever sit down and look at a guy and say, "does this guy have grade 12 or university education? Does he have 15 years experience in the business?" We never look at that side of the person, we look for good people first. And then we'll train the people to do what we want. I guess we can train people to do that, but we can't train people to be good people.

Manager, Mayo Forest Products

Mediocrity is not good enough—especially in joint ventures that aim for competitiveness on a global scale. To meet strategic demands in the joint ventures, exemplary staff who possess both personal and technical skills are hired into all levels of the venture. Both hourly and salaried employees are selected based on their ability to communicate, learn new skills, and operate as team members. In some cases, personal skills are more important than technical abilities.

Previous experience is not always necessary. For example, at Diamond Star, employees without previous experience in an automotive manufacturing setting are deliberately hired, in anticipation that they will be more open to novel ideas and new ways of operating on the job. The Manager for Quality Circles at Diamond Star mentions that when he and others went to Japan for training in the early days of the venture, they expected to be placed in jobs similar to those in which they had previously worked. Instead, many placements were made based on potential rather than past experience.

Screening processes are extensive, and at Diamond Star production associates are hired through an assessment center, a format more usually used for hiring of executive talent. In the other ventures, selection is completed by selection committees. To exchange managerial and technical competencies between the JV and parent firms, both temporary employee transfers and more permanent staff placements from the parent firm are widely utilized.

The emphasis on staffing at Mayo Forest Products, OCG, Siecor, and Diamond Star is in contrast to previous research on international joint ventures. In a review of the literature on joint ventures, Shenkar and Zeira (1987) found that in 12 of 19 studies on JV firms, a gap existed between actual and desired levels of staffing in the venture. Although there is no definitive answer why there is so much focus on high-quality staffing in the four joint ventures described here, one might speculate that this emphasis reinforces the JV strategic objectives. In each of the ventures (all of which have been very successful in product excellence and innovation), quality staff with broad skills are required in order that they can be rotated to various positions as well as contribute new ideas. High-quality production staff are especially critical to this process.

Further, if companies are to realize strategic objectives, then sufficient numbers of staff are required to complete tasks effectively. Staffing that is too lean will have detrimental effects on both employees and the operation of the venture. Excessive overtime and multiple shifts can result in deterioration of employee health. At Diamond Star, where production demands have escalated in recent years, there are more staff off work with injuries. In addition, because staffing is lean, there is less time for production staff to devote to Kaizen and Quality Circles that ultimately contribute to the realization of JV objectives. Within the HR department at Diamond Star, various managers note that they require more HR staff in order to be proactive, and to keep up with demands for timely new policy. Given these considerations, not only do competitive companies require high calibre staff, but they also need them in sufficient numbers.

THE SELECTION OF PRODUCTION ASSOCIATES

Although to some extent hiring of production associates is accomplished in traditional ways (e.g., advertisements, application forms, interviews), more creative staffing variations are also used in the four joint ventures described here. For instance, at Siecor, hiring is increasingly done by the associates themselves. Recruitment of production employees is done through an assessment center at Diamond Star.

To elaborate, in keeping with a strategy of employee involvement at Siecor, the hiring committee that evaluates temporary employees for permanent positions is comprised of production associates. Associate selection is based on a "mentor review" completed by a prospective employee's peers who consider supervisor's ratings and attendance records. Although hiring of production employees by peer review is not prevalent in industry, this system worked well at Siecor. Responsibility for staff selection is given to employees who know the job best, and who will eventually interact with the prospective candidate. This system of peer selection is likely to have maximum benefit when training in selection procedures is provided to employees responsible for this task.

At Diamond Star, the assessment center was developed by a consulting company with input from the Japanese. In the early stages of setting up the assessment format, members of the consulting company went to Japan to observe Japanese methods, and to talk with workers and managers in the Mitsubishi plant. Interviews were held with Japanese managers already transferred to Diamond Star. The consultants also spoke to Americans about what it is like to build a car and work in an auto manufacturing facility. Following the completion of this preliminary groundwork, the assessment criteria and hiring procedures were determined.

Individuals who are to be considered as prospective employees for Diamond Star are initially prescreened by the local employment office and given the General Aptitude Test Battery (GATB). An individual generally needs to score in the 70th percentile or higher to remain in the screening process. Successful candidates are then referred to the assessment center for further testing. They undergo the Bennett Mechanical Aptitude Test and a group exercise. For the exercise, applicants perform a group activity, and assessors observe the process to determine how well individuals are able to function as part of the group. Diamond Star candidates undergo a physical examination and a drug screen. The final step in the assessment process is a standardized interview. Candidates who proceed to the interview stage have a 95 percent chance of being hired.

Diamond Star management prefer to have about 100 people in a "ready to hire pool" in order that additional staff can be quickly recruited when required. Generally, staffing at Diamond Star has been "lean," and employees are working more overtime and double shifts than they did in the early days at the plant. There are no temporary workers at Diamond Star. A group of 56 permanent employees fill in when needed, although the chairman of the bargaining committee feels this should be a larger group. As with other Japanese-influenced plants, there is a no layoff policy in practice. One HR manager mentions they had hired a number of new employees who were still in a probationary period when the company experienced a downturn in schedule. Rather than terminate staff, which he comments would have been typical in an American-style factory, all new staff remained with Diamond Star.

Based on the selection procedure, the associates at Diamond Star are relatively young and well educated. The average level of education is 14 years and reflects the requirement for a highly skilled workforce which can rotate to various positions in the plant. There are only two job classifications (as opposed to 60 or 70 in some plants), so associates are needed with "interchangeable qualifications." As one manager notes, the associates have high expectations for advancement, and some have become frustrated due to an inability to move to supervisory positions. This is the case despite considerable upward movement of plant employees. Another manager notes that in retrospect it would have been a good idea to hire some people who would be satisfied with more routine activities. He adds the physical demands of the manufacturing operation are considerable, and currently employees undergo a complex physical examination.

SPECIAL REQUIREMENTS FOR JOINT VENTURE MANAGERS

JV managers must be visionaries and politicians. They need to have a good knowledge of the business, and of the strategy and cultures of the parent firms. They must be able to balance the priorities and demands of the joint venture as well as of the parents, and to develop trust. A senior executive at Mayo Forest Products outlines the role of the JV General Manager.

You must recognize you have two owners, even if one is only five percent ownership. It's still an owner, still has rights, still ought to be given opportunities. . . . So joint venture managers of this world need to be prepared to deal with the vagaries and the nuisance factors of having two separate owners from two separate cultures who ask two entirely different sets of questions . . . and have different levels of expectations. . . . So to be a good general manager, you have to have supreme objectivity at all times, whether it's dealing with an employee or some other stakeholder, or a competitor, or whatever. It might be a customer. With the owners you need a much higher level of sensitivity and awareness—but it really comes down to understanding, tolerance, patience . . . and they [the owners] have to get to the point where they trust you. And if your owner doesn't trust you then the relationship won't exist very long.

The General Manager at Mayo Forest Products adds that it is important for him to have a "good understanding of the politics of the business." He notes it is a very dangerous game to play one partner against the other, even though at times the temptation to do so exists.

Because good "personal chemistry at the top" was acknowledged by managers as essential to the operation of the JV-parent interface, senior staff ideally possess good communication skills and interpersonal relationship abilities, and are open to new ideas. Additional assets are international management experience, adaptability, and ability to speak multiple languages. Credibility is very important. A senior manager at Siecor comments,

Credibility has to encompass all the partners in the joint venture and the employees in the organization. It's probably, I think, the single most critical element. If you have a lot of credibility as an individual . . . you have to then establish your credibility with the folks at Siemens, in our case with the folks at Corning, and with the people who work on the shop floor and with the people who work above you. And if you're working within the joint venture if you lose that credibility with any of those four, any single one of those four, it greatly impairs your ability to accomplish your tasks.

With regard to the qualities required of an HR manager in a joint venture, one executive mentions the importance of being able to resist pressure from the parents to conform to policies which may not be appropriate for the joint venture. "It's very easy to be swept away on the tide of corporate policies from outside giants." Another manager observes that an HR manager must be "open minded, willing to communicate, and able to communicate . . . and maybe do things differently than you've done them in the past." He adds that it is important to "take the initiative to understand the individual businesses that we're in. And you have to be able to communicate that knowledge that you acquire, and ask the astute questions."

Managerial talent assigned to the joint venture must be top rate, and not conveniently sent to the venture as a way to rid the parent of unwanted executives. Although at Siecor transfers from one parent are now approved by the other, there was a time when employees were sent to the venture who were highly paid but not essential to the business. A Siecor executive remarks,

Frankly, some of the people who came down [to Siecor] were highly paid. And when you've got high-paid people that really nobody understands their function or their role, they're really not needed by the business, at least in the other parent's perception, right? It's half their [Siemens's] money, they're paying half their salary and it's almost that simple. But those were the growing pains. In all honesty, we went through that phase.

In joint ventures with the Japanese, managers are selected based on implicit criteria, and a dedication to and belief in Japanese management and manufacturing philosophy. One Japanese Vice-President at Diamond Star explains that in the hiring process, "Wa, you know, the harmony, is important . . . not how good you are, not how good your abilities or skills may be." Managers are hired based on the concept of "face"—the unspoken chemistry of how sincere and loyal the person is perceived to be.

Senior Japanese managers who were involved in the establishment of selection procedures at Diamond Star note the importance of a "manager's subjective judgment" in choosing a job candidate. For both associate and manager groups the Japanese managers prefer to introduce implicit evaluation criteria (e.g., the ability to have harmonious relationships with others), rather than rely on objective point ratings. One Japanese manager said it is impossible for him to judge people based on standardized criteria because "everything should be a thousand cases." Therefore each case needs to be evaluated differently.

The underlying philosophy of an American manager to union-management relations is important to the Japanese. Flexibility is a key element. The HR General Manager (who is American) at Diamond Star described his interview with Japanese managers in Japan,

They wanted to know if my philosophies were set to the traditional automotive [factory], or was I going to be able to adapt to new concepts, new ideas, and try and build something new. Or was I going to just be what they [the Japanese] figured was the traditional American management style, nonparticipative, you're going to do it my way, we're not going to listen to you.

The issue which the HR General Manager repeatedly addressed during his interviews in Japan was his position on labor, and whether he intended to fight with or cooperate with the union.

TRANSFERS FOR LEARNING

Transfers of staff between the JV and the parent firms can provide a mechanism for sharing information, for learning from each other's abilities and expertise, and for the creation of synergies related to product development. Flexibility is built into the operation by the temporary transfer of staff to work on projects, who then return to the parent once they are no longer required in the joint venture. In joint ventures in which there is little or no transfer of employees, opportunities for the parent and JV staff to learn from each other may be lost. This is especially the case when technical exchanges have the potential to enhance products and systems in the joint venture. Related to this, Collins and Doorley (1991: 114) suggest, "the key to transferring detailed technical knowledge, and applying it commercially, is people." The authors add that this might best be accomplished by medium- to long-term assignment of parent personnel to the venture.

Except at Mayo Forest Products, the joint ventures have large numbers of managerial and technical staff either permanently reassigned or on loan to the venture from the parent companies. Transfers are for a significant period of time—usually three to five years. An advantage of staffing the joint venture with members from the parent firms is that linkages from the venture to the parent are already established. Communication may be facilitated when transferred employees already know whom to contact in the parent organizations for information or assistance, and have already developed a working rapport with other parent employees.

Large numbers of parent employees in the joint venture are able to bring parent influence to the venture, and subsequently, the development of an identity unique to the venture becomes problematic. The parent with management responsibility may draw on a wide range of parent policies, including HR policies or other HR support. A manager at Siecor mentions, "It's probably true to say that from a general standpoint, the number of parent employees that are brought in [to the JV] probably has a big influence on how, and how fast, the joint venture grows, what it looks like, and what kind of culture it has." In support of this statement, Frayne and Geringer (1989) suggest that the control of JV operations by managers from the parent firm is related to the number of parent staff in the venture, and their particular assignments.

Another transfer issue relates to the advantages of permanent reassignment of employees (managers, technical personnel), versus temporary transfers. As already suggested, temporary transfers provide maximal operational flexibility. Alternately, permanently-assigned employees (or employees hired directly to the joint venture), may have a greater commitment to the operation. At Diamond Star, managers who are hired directly to the venture take special pride in their status as "Diamond Star employees" rather than being "dispatchees" from one of the parents. For employees who are permanently located in the venture, their livelihood depends on JV success. This is especially true if policies are not in place where JV staff can easily transfer to the parent organization, and take all their seniority and benefits with them. Further, the degree of loyalty employees feel toward the venture may be negatively affected if better employment prospects are perceived to exist in the parent company. Whether or not carry-over policies should exist for employees who wish to permanently relocate from the parent firms to the joint venture is a complex issue. If no carry-over policies exist, then employees may feel somewhat "trapped" in the venture, as they did at OCG. This has the long-term effect of reduced morale and employee contributions. At Diamond Star, if an employee chooses to leave the parent and permanently transfer to the venture, then he or she severs previous company ties and begins anew to accumulate benefits and seniority. An HR manager at Diamond Star says this policy was intentional, and aims to create "allegiance all to the joint venture company, not to the parent company." The opposite occurs at Siecor, where each parent treats the transfer of employees to the joint venture as if the employee continues to work for the parent.

If employees experience difficulty in rejoining the parent firm once they have been on assignment to the joint venture, then talented employees may be discouraged from leaving the parent for the venture. At OCG, employees who decided to join the joint venture could not bid back to the parent for a period of two years, in order to ensure the stability of the venture. As a result, getting employees to volunteer for JV assignments was very difficult. Alternately, if an abundance of tangible benefits exists for staff who transfer to the joint venture (e.g., special retirement benefits, various financial perks), then implicitly this may send a signal to employees that it is more desirable to work in the parent firm, with the incentives provided having the appearance of "isolation pay."

Theoretically, JV assignments can provide great opportunities for employees to gain broader, often international expertise in a new environment. This potentially adds value to employee credentials. If managers in the parent strive to tie transferred employees' career advancement in the parent to high-level performance in the venture, then parent employees may view the JV assignment as a chance to gain valuable experience which is ultimately linked to their career advancement. Typically such coupling was not initiated at Mayo, OCG, Siecor, or Diamond Star.

CAREER PATHING AND PROMOTIONS

When managers withhold information from employees regarding career opportunities (or make decisions independent of employee input), employee responsibility related to career self-development is greatly reduced. A relative absence of job postings and other career-related information is problematic for employees who perceive they have limited information related to jobs for which they are qualified. Ideally, promotion criteria will be clearly stated and communicated to employees to prevent career blocking.

When no job postings exist, some employees view career or promotional systems as unfair. In the absence of employee input, managers decide the jobs for which their staff might best be suited. Implicitly this process assumes that managers or supervisors are both aware of employee interests and capabilities, and are equally aware of all relevant career opportunities in the organization. For managers with narrow functional experience this is unlikely to be the case. As one manager at Siecor remarks, "What I think we fail to recognize is that there are a lot of managers in this company who have no cross-functional experience who would have a very difficult time explaining to people what other jobs are out there."

At Diamond Star, an American HR manager's proposed system of job postings was "killed by the Japanese general managers" who felt the program would take selection decision-making out of their hands. Consequently, employees "don't know what's open, when it's open." On one occasion a DSM production manager advertised for a position in the community newspaper and received a "flood" of applications from employees already working at Diamond Star. One production associate explains, "when there's an opening they call down to the group leader and ask him to submit some names of who he would like to see promoted. That's it." He adds,

We would like to have more information. But one thing we can not figure out is how they evaluate you to promote you. There's no set scale. One branch manager will make up a rule to get the person promoted he wants. Another one will have just the opposite point of view.

In the case of managerial development at Siecor, promotions are decided informally. A manager notes,

Negotiations are usually in a bar room between two competing managers off site. I can offer this person this. What can you offer him? I think to a great extent people would like to see all jobs posted so we would have a bidding process for all jobs regardless of level. I think the practical aspect of that is I don't want that to happen. It seems too inefficient.

In joint ventures, when career paths may extend beyond the boundaries of the venture to include the parent firms as well, the possibility that managers are unaware of employee career opportunities is heightened. A formal career development process and widespread job postings become even more imperative.

Somewhat unusual, at Siecor career planning programs for production or technical staff are better developed than for managers. As part of the program, the Myers-Briggs personality test is administered to employees to help them identify their personality characteristics and where their interests and skills lie relative to available jobs within the company. In addition, the HR department has grouped jobs at Siecor in order that employees can determine within a matrix which jobs might be most suitable. Job descriptions are grouped together by "families." Employees are informed they can make appointments with the personnel managers to discuss career development.

LESSONS LEARNED

In all the joint ventures, the quality of employees is a priority. In some instances, having the right personal skills is more important than technical background and competency. Employees tend to be hired based on their ability to communicate and learn new skills, and on whether or not they can operate as part of the team.

To maximize the people potential in the ventures, staffing ideally involves:

1. extensive screening procedures for employees at all levels;
2. exchange of staff from the parents who are strong contributors with appropriate skill sets (versus "deadwood" that the parent firms wanted to relocate);
3. allocation of sufficient numbers of staff to the joint venture to maximize the benefits of continuous improvement through high employee involvement;
4. hiring managers to the joint venture with special skills beyond those of traditional managers (e.g., possessing cultural and political expertise as well as knowledge of management techniques);
5. staffing at "the top" (e.g., the JV Board) with managers who have exemplary personal skills, the ability to communicate effectively, and flexibility; and
6. the development of HR policy that protects the interests of the joint venture (e.g., retain key JV personnel) but at the same time allows flexibility in order that staff don't feel trapped in the venture.

CHAPTER 10

Training and Development Priorities

To succeed we need people—innovative, skilled and well trained to meet all the requirements of our jobs.

General Manager, Mayo Forest Products

Training is a major emphasis at Mayo Forest Products, OCG, Siecor, and Diamond Star. Training is wide-based and often involves cross-training of production staff in order to build flexibility into the manufacturing operation. Training focuses on both personal and technical skills. In addition, training is sometimes provided on company strategy or the parent cultures, in order that employees are able to better identify with the venture. The extensive amount of training provided to employees seems to be worthwhile, and both associates and managers feel they are sufficiently qualified to perform their jobs. When problem-solving and teamwork are important, training might be expected to focus on these components, although this was not evident in the four ventures. Training is provided both on-the-job and in the classroom, and, in general, both time and resources are adequately committed. In some instances, training is more extensive for production associates than for managers.

VARIETY IN TRAINING PROGRAMS

Training for salaried staff (e.g., supervisors, managers) in all the joint ventures is wide-based and generally available. For example, at Mayo Forest Products salaried employees receive training in technical, supervisory and interpersonal skills. OCG provides TQM training, as well as teamwork, interpersonal, and supervisory training. Siecor has training in interpersonal skills, communication, technical areas, and quality management; the goal is to provide managerial and administrative/technical staff with 40 hours of training per year. At Diamond Star, managers and supervisors receive training in Japanese management and production methods, performance appraisal, computers, project management, and supervisory training. Much of the training is offered internally—either by the JV training department or in parent training facilities. Salaried staff are more likely to receive off-site training provided by external sources than are production staff.

Managers in all joint ventures stress the importance of training to enhance employee teamwork and production quality. Training for production employees is mostly on-the-job, but other opportunities for training are offered. At Mayo Forest Products considerable time, energy, and expense are devoted to the creation of a competency-based, on-the-job training program for production workers. Comprehensive training manuals for each job station were developed by equipment operators and an outside consultant. To become qualified for a job, production staff complete a written test and a performance test, and then undergo a qualifying period when a skills checklist is used to ensure the job has been adequately learned. In addition, production workers at Mayo are eligible for classroom training in specific, job-related areas (e.g., quality, maximizing lumber recovery) and are paid to attend the classes.

Training for production employees at OCG is on-the-job, and there is a manual of standard operating procedures for all jobs in the plant. When learning a new job, a skills checklist is completed by employees and supervisors to guarantee the job has been learned properly.

In each of Siecor's plants, training resource people work in conjunction with the Training Director at the corporate office. Production associates provide instruction for their peers once they have successfully completed "train the trainer" programs. Associates receive some cross-training and team member training in keeping with the company philosophy of high employee involvement. Team member training includes business awareness, communication skills, group dynamics, conflict management, group development, and personality typing on the Myers-Briggs personality test. The "total team building concept" incorporates a discussion about managing change, and an explanation of why changes in the plant are occurring. Associate teams decide which members of their group will go to training, and determine the training schedule. Associates feel they receive more than adequate training and one comments, "It [training] is continuous, it never stops. We never stop learning."

A cross-functional group of associates is beginning to develop a new system for training in one of Siecor's plants. Under the system, on-the-job training performance of an individual is evaluated by peers. Points are assigned for level of skill accomplishment. As an associate earns points, he or she will progress through various training stages, until the maximal number of skills is learned. Eventually the number of skills an associate possesses will determine salary levels.

At Diamond Star, large numbers of coordinators and technical assistants were transferred to the venture from Mitsubishi to provide training in Japanese management philosophy and production methods to American production workers. Alternately, 26 maintenance associates, who later assumed the responsibilities of group leaders, spent ten months training in Japan. In addition, in the early stages of the joint venture, approximately 300 managers and supervisors at Diamond Star who are American received training in Japan. Quality circle training, which is an important component of training for production associates, is provided by an American who spent considerable time in Japan learning QC methods. Although training is also provided at Diamond Star from external sources, at present this is fairly limited.

CULTURAL TRAINING

Cultural training in the ventures can encompass (1) the corporate norms and values which operate in the company, and with which employees may eventually identify, and (2) language and other training related to the creation of a better understanding of the national culture of the parents or off-shore customers.

More specifically, in some of the ventures training is provided to employees about the company strategic mission, JV history and traditions, the business environment in which the joint venture operates, and how to manage and understand change. For example, at Siecor a course is provided called "Siecor Environment," related to how the company operates in the technological environment. Also at Siecor, associates and supervisors receive training in how to manage changing roles in the plant, and why changes have occurred. The transition is most difficult for supervisors. As the Training Director remarks, "they [supervisors] are the ones that really get hit in the crunch . . . it can be very devastating. [We need] to let them know that they're going to win by being leaders instead of bosses." Although training about corporate transition is generally not offered in most companies, the information seemed valuable to employees in order that they make better sense of the work environment.

Training related to the corporate culture can be offered in orientation sessions provided to new employees (Cascio and Serapio, 1991). At Mayo Forest Products the orientation includes safety, the quality emphasis in the company, and an identification of the people who work in the operation. The employee handbook which is given to new employees provides a brief history of the joint venture arrangement of the company. At Diamond Star, the employee orientation includes a plant tour, an explanation of employee benefits, and a briefing about the various departments.

An important consideration for JV managers is which parent values and styles will predominate in the venture, or whether the intent is to create a unique corporate culture for the venture, separate from the parents. Based on who provides training, different priorities and values will be passed to employees. If one parent provides most of the training, then it is likely that certain operating norms and values will be transferred to JV employees by either trainers or training materials associated with that parent. At OCG, training content and other "cultural information" given to JV employees has on it the name of the parent firm. JV employees indicated some resentment toward this practice, especially when they have been absorbed into the venture from the non-dominant parent company.

A second form of cultural training—related to the parent national cultures—was available to employees in three of the four joint ventures. At Mayo Forest Products a five-year training plan includes courses in the Japanese market, culture, and certification standards. A course in the German language is offered at Siecor, although few employees have taken advantage of the program. Employees transferred from Siecor to Germany for a period of several years are eligible for a course about German culture, history, and politics. Eight hours of cultural training (e.g., Japanese customs, culture, business practices, language) was originally offered to Diamond Star employees; however, this program was ended once an initial subsidy offered to the Japanese parent for location in Illinois ran out. In all cases, training was offered related only to the offshore parent culture.

When more than one national cultural is represented in the joint venture, there are advantages to providing training to employees of *both* cultural groups about the cultures and languages that operate in the venture. In joint ventures, the importance of multiple language skills and international management skills cannot be diminished. Somewhat surprising, none of the ventures emphasized training related to the specific skills required of international managers, or how the JV-parent relationship can be managed. Managers may be encouraged to attain these skills if they are linked to promotions and other career progressions.

In the instances where training about national culture is offered, the material is not generally provided in a forum which allows for the *active* integration of cultural information. For example, training content is typically provided in a classroom setting, without an opportunity for participants to discuss differences and similarities between the national cultures represented in the venture. If JV members are to gain enhanced cultural understanding, then ideally an action learning model will operate in which employees explore cultural values, accepted processes or policies, and cultural interpretations. This form of cultural analysis is especially appropriate for managers in joint ventures and other multicultural settings, who seek knowledge related to the diverse processes which operate among cultural groups. However, as Jaeger (1986) notes, the format of interventions themselves are subject to the influence of cultural expectations of the participants.

A senior manager for training at Siemens' headquarters office in Germany believes that the creation of cross-cultural understanding is very important in the context of joint ventures and other forms of strategic alliances. This manager and others at Siemens headquarters have formed a team that focuses specifically on the development of training programs to enhance cultural communication and understanding among different cultural groups within a given venture. Training programs are provided to managers in the alliances to enhance an appreciation of the partner's culture—and to avoid cultural misunderstanding. According to the Siemens manager, this form of training has been essential to the success of the companies with which he has been involved. The absence of a similar training function in other international companies is striking. The success of this program indicates that in other companies, a focus on better cultural understanding among the partners deserves wider consideration.

JOB ROTATION IN PRODUCTION FACILITIES

Job rotation is a system in which employees rotate to various jobs in order to gain broad skills. The benefit to the employee is greater job variety, and less potential for boredom as the result of repetitive job assignments. The benefit to the company is greater flexibility in the manufacturing process. Regarding the four joint ventures described here, job rotation does not operate at Mayo Forest Products, is used minimally at OCG, operates primarily in the experimental work teams in the plants at Siecor, and is used at Diamond Star. Although job rotation in theory has positive benefits, in practice it may be too expensive for companies to operate. Another pitfall of job rotation is that favoritism on the part of supervisors may prevent production employees from having equal opportunities to train in all relevant job stations.

To elaborate, a production employee at Mayo Forest Products explains that job rotation may incur extra costs for the company. In sawmills where he knew job rotation did operate, an employee may work three different jobs (one week in each job), and is paid the top rate for all three positions. In an economy where job turnover in the lumber industry is virtually nil, there exists little incentive for companies to increase costs to retain employees.

Further, at Diamond Star, some associates note that preferred jobs like those off-line or in robotics are selectively assigned by supervisors. Thus not all employees have the opportunity to work at all jobs. If job rotation does not operate consistently, then employees may come to quickly distrust the motives of managers—resulting in long-term job dissatisfaction and reduced motivation. A production worker remarks,

> It's not like they promised everybody in the beginning. They [management] promised you equal training and full rotation of jobs, and they came to find out for some of these jobs that some people can't do or don't want to do the job. And there are other jobs that they won't let people do because they are preferred jobs and they hand pick who they want to put on those. And everybody [the associates] was under the impression that they would rotate through all aspects of the team concept here. And that just doesn't work. They [management] found out it's not practical for them to implement that because of the building of the cars and they have to have X number of cars built a day, and if they have to train everybody all the time they weren't getting their production out.

In practice, then, when production schedules are a pressing concern for managers, less emphasis may be placed on training employees in multiple job skills or job rotation. In more technical positions there is an advantage to keeping employees in a single job because they gain more specialized experience. When production demands escalate, some production employees complain they received reduced training and that less time is available for employees to meet and discuss quality improvements. Consequently, the strategic operating goals of the company related to continuous improvement and employee involvement are not sustained. To some extent, then, rigorous production schedules and systems that encourage high employee involvement are mutually exclusive. Managers must determine their priorities related to maximum product output, versus other issues such as product quality or employee job satisfaction.

LESSONS LEARNED

Training receives top priority in competitive international joint ventures. Training is wide-based for all employees, and in some cases training is more extensive for production staff than for managers and supervisors. In addition to technical and interpersonal training, cultural training in either corporate values and norms or national culture is a welcome addition to helping employees understand the organization of which they are a part.

Although this sample of joint ventures exhibited many strengths in their training programs, there are some areas where improvement is warranted:

- a greater emphasis on the acquisition of multiple language skills and international management skills is desirable;
- more focus should be placed on active rather than passive learning;

- in instances where job rotation is implemented as a way to train in broad skills, rotation must be fairly implemented in practice; and
- managers must be able to balance production demands with the need to allow employees time off the floor to acquire promised training.

CHAPTER 11

Meaningful Reward and Recognition Systems

I think it [recognition programs] work . . . in really all types of areas—
in safety as well as work performance on the floor. It's just a type of
recognition, and that's what you need basically on the floor—to know
that the work that you're doing is appreciated, and that they [man-
agement] are looking at you.

Production Associate, Diamond Star

Rewards are a powerful incentive for augmented work performance, and
can be used to reinforce the strategic agenda in the venture. TQM, product innovation, and teamwork are important goals; however, only sporad-
ically are rewards offered in alignment with employee accomplishments
specifically tied to strategy. For example, if a goal in manufacturing facilities is to develop team activities, then rewards should be provided to
employees for team, rather than individual, performance. Instead, rewards
are more likely provided for individual rather than group performance.

Further, managers find the creation and implementation of meaningful
recognition systems a challenge. To be most meaningful, recognition is
linked to employee performance, individually valued by employees, and
consistently applied.

GOALS OF REWARD SYSTEMS

The purpose of monetary compensation is to attract, motivate, and retain employees. In competitive joint venture companies, ideally compensation systems are structured to reward employees for product improve-

ments and work performance that exceed normal work requirements. The compensation system "emphasizes the individuality and distinctive competencies of each person, with pay allocated for knowledge and performance" (Forward et al. 1991: 39). Reward incentives for employees that are linked to learning and innovation are most likely to result in the creation of new solutions, or changes to products or processes which ultimately benefit the firm. In competitive companies in which rewards are not given for high employee performance in these areas, inconsistency exists between stated policy and policy in action.

At Mayo Forest Products, OCG, Siecor, and Diamond Star, pay is variably linked to performance—especially for hourly employees. For instance at Mayo Forest Products, where the strategic emphasis is on a high-performance management system, the monetary reward system for hourly employees is fixed by the union contract. Monetary compensation for special individual performance or team efforts are generally lacking. At Diamond Star, which is also unionized, no bonuses are tied to productivity, although the HR department was considering the implementation of this form of program. To some extent, incentive plans have not been introduced at Diamond Star because, as one American manager explains, "the whole idea of monetary rewards and things like that is definitely against the Japanese way of doing things." Instead through the use of Kaizen, improvements are initiated that make the job easier, safer, and more interesting for employees. This manager adds that most Kaizens cost the company money, as well as implicitly offer rewards to employees. Alternately, OCG has Quality awards of small cash amounts for quality performance. At Siecor, in the future production associates will be offered financial incentives for high levels of performance.

COMPENSATION FOR MANAGERS AND EXECUTIVES

For managerial or other salaried staff, incentive programs also tend to be limited. At Mayo Forest Products, good performance is rewarded by annual salary increases that are subjective, and based on a "gut feel" of how the direct superior thinks the employee performs. OCG provides financial bonuses for mid-level managers or higher, while Siecor has unit cash awards for salaried staff provided on an individual basis. Salary policies at Siecor are "identical" to those of the American parent according to a manager in Human Resources. At both OCG and Siecor, where innovation and creativity are desired, some rewards exist for technological accomplishments. Diamond Star provides an across-the-board annual bonus for managers which is not tied to performance. At the executive level, compensation which is tied to JV success provides incentives for managers to concentrate on the viability of the venture (Frayne and Geringer, 1989). However, this form of executive compensation was not usually applied in the joint ventures described here. Without incentives that are tied to venture performance, executives or other managers (who may experience divided loyalty to the joint venture and the parent anyway) may be tempted to spend more time making career connections back to the parent firm than to stimulating successes in the joint venture. Financial rewards can also be a powerful tool to encourage cooperation among technical staff, task force groups, and other cross-functional teams having JV and parent staff. If various incentives for joint project success are available to employees, then technological sharing, innovation based on combined expertise from parent groups, and project successes may be more likely to flourish. Reward systems that are designed to suit the unique orientation of the venture, as opposed to those taken whole or piecemeal from the parent firms, may be the most effective.

MULTIPLE COMPENSATION SYSTEMS

In international joint ventures, more than one compensation system sometimes may operate simultaneously. Executives or other employees transferred to the venture may remain on the payroll of the parent firm. In addition, a separate compensation system might be developed for JV staff. At OCG, Siecor, and Diamond Star, more than one compensation system is in operation. More specifically, at OCG R&D staff from the Swiss parent are designated as JV staff, but are leased to the venture; they remain on the Ciba-Geigy payroll and benefit systems, and costs to the parent are billed back to OCG. At Diamond Star, a large number of upper level executives who remain employees of either Chrysler or Mitsubishi are paid by the parent. At both Siecor and Diamond Star, technical staff on temporary loan to the joint venture continue to be paid by the parent firm.

According to Cascio and Serapio (1991: 71), multiple compensation systems may have a negative impact on staff in international alliances. They write,

Failure to establish a uniform compensation policy in an international alliance that requires high interaction among employees from different partners can lead to predictably adverse effects. Differences in compensation systems, especially for employees doing the same jobs, often lead to feelings of inequity among those receiving lower compensation and benefits. Morale and motivation therefore suffer among group members.

However, contrary to these predictions, multiple compensation arrangements did not seem problematic for JV staff at Mayo, OCG, Siecor, or Diamond Star. Generally, JV employees knew different reward systems existed, but felt that as long as an individual remained under the parent umbrella, he or she was considered in a different category. Further, most staff were not aware of actual salary differences that existed. What appeared to be more important to employees in judging the fairness of their compensation systems was whether reward systems were *consistently* applied *within* the group of employees officially designated to the joint venture. This was more significant to JV employees than the manner in which staff on temporary assignment from the parent were rewarded. Related to this, if reward incentives appear inconsistent within a department in the joint venture, then staff are likely to be dissatisfied. For example, at Siecor, different awards are available to sales versus marketing staff, and this has been a source of discontent for marketing employees who perceive they are not able to make as much money as their counterparts in sales.

AN EMPHASIS ON NON-MONETARY RECOGNITION

As is the case with monetary reward systems, non-monetary recognition systems in progressive companies are instituted to recognize excellence in employee performance. Recognition demonstrates to employees that their efforts are appreciated, and consequently encourages continued excellence. If recognition programs are to be consistent with a teamwork approach, then recognition should be provided for group effort and accomplishments. This does not preclude the existence of individual recognition as well. Generally, despite stated team objectives, recognition is given for individual rather than team efforts.

An interesting feature of the joint ventures described here is the large number of recognition programs in effect, and the creativity of their conception. For example, at Mayo Forest Products, recognition may include verbal praise, dinners, trips, trophies, jackets, thank you letters, gift certificates, or donuts. When the saw-filing department achieved seven years without a lost time injury, the department supervisor sent seven long-stemmed roses to the home of each member of his crew.

The recognition system is not lip service at Mayo, but is enacted at every opportunity by managers and supervisors. In addition to performance recognition in the JV newsletter, expressions of praise are often heard at the many meetings attended by managers, supervisors, and other employees. Recognition is given to individuals or groups in production meetings for work well done or a good "team effort."

At OCG, employees are recognized for their performance in the newsletter. In addition, there are recognition dinners to honor employees for accomplishments, pizza days to celebrate record days of production, and dinner certificates for employees who excel. Siecor offers recognition to employees in various forms including: employee of the quarter and employee of the year; Total Quality Management defect preventer of the year; inventor of the year; and a president's sales club for employees who excel in sales performance. Since 1987, a PRAISE program has operated under which employees can nominate their peers for either small or more significant contributions to the company. For each nomination, employees receive a voucher worth three dollars which is redeemable in the company cafeteria or store. Employees who are recognized under the PRAISE program have their names posted on the Peer Recognition board in the cafeteria. On their birthdays, employees receive a balloon and a candy apple at the corporate office.

At Siecor's plants, recognition programs have been initiated by both managers and production associates. A plant manager remarks, "We try to do quite a lot with recognition and they're all home grown." The aim is to have "little and often" and to "try to recognize successes when we can." Recognition varies from free soft drinks on a given day for reduced "scrap" levels to a free meal. The employee of the month is chosen by peer review and receives a cash award, a T-shirt, and a plaque, and has preferred parking near the front door for a month. An employee who wins this recognition is automatically put on a list for employee of the year and is eligible for more cash and other prizes and preferred parking for a year. Other forms of recognition include a "Dinner for Two" program, shirts, and luncheons. When employees complete a training class they get a framed certificate.

At Diamond Star, there are no employee recognition programs except for those based on quality circle performance. Although in general Japanese managers do not favor a recognition system, some American managers note that there should be small gifts and other forms of recognition available to employees for no lost time or project accomplishments. One American manager mentions that Americans are different from the Japanese and appreciate "public acknowledgement" for achievements. An associate at Diamond Star concurs that he would like to see more recognition of employees, "to know that the work that you're doing is appreciated, and that they [management] are looking at you." In view of these comments, there is some evidence that the Japanese management preferences in the plant may need to be revised in the area of recognition, in order to accommodate the expectations of American workers. The HR department can have a role in the creation of new recognition programs, but first it needs assurances that the application of these programs will have plant-wide approval, including that of the Japanese managers.

RECOGNITION FOR SAFETY

In all the joint ventures except Diamond Star, recognition was provided to employees for safe work performance, and was withheld from employees who had on-the-job accidents. Although safety was a priority in all the ventures, the merits of providing recognition and/or monetary reward in this area are not clear. In fact, according to traditional reinforcement theory, the withholding of reward is considered "negative reinforcement." In companies where recognition in the form of "safety bucks" is given for safe work performance, the withholding of safety recognition and rewards is an incentive for employees to conceal on-the-job injuries. Further, when safety recognition is for groups rather than for individual on-the-job safety, employees who report injuries may feel as though they are contributing to the loss of recognition for their entire group. Some of their peers may perceive this also, and in some instances employees avoided reporting minor injuries in order to maintain a safe work record.

At Mayo Forest Products, one production worker explains, "I got a little bonk on the head and I went to first aid and got it checked out there and then I didn't get my 15 dollars. And that made me mad. . . . I don't like that incentive . . . everybody is then hiding their little sprains and bruises." When recognition for safety is provided only if there are no accidents in a unit or group, then peer pressure is placed on individuals who have an accident, thereby blemishing the safety record of the entire group. One associate at Siecor mentions that although members of a group should implicitly be concerned for one another's safety, reward or recognition for safety should be based only on individual performance.

THE CREATION OF MEANINGFUL RECOGNITION SYSTEMS

It is interesting that despite the general emphasis on recognition programs, managers felt the implementation of effective programs remained problematic. In support of this idea, managers at Mayo Forest Products feel one of the biggest challenges they face is the creation of *meaningful* employee recognition systems. The General Manager at Mayo remarks, "the appreciation for people is paramount and to encourage and recognize improvements in performance and never, never, try to buy performance." However, in some cases employees were not always informed or aware of the reason for recognition, diluting its reinforcement value. At Siecor, a manager remarks, "a lot of the employees are uncomfortable being recognized as the employee of the quarter because in a lot of cases they don't really understand why." This suggests that if recognition programs are to have maximal value, then employees need a clear concept of what the programs involve, and why recognition is offered.

Some employees stated that they like to be recognized; others felt the recognition was an embarrassment. Related to this, the effect of recognition programs varies greatly depending on individual employee preferences. For this reason, managers must consider what is appropriate recognition for either an individual or a group. Although considerable time is spent on the development of recognition programs, there is little evidence that managers spend time tailoring reinforcements to be appropriate for specific individuals or groups. Further, if managers do not use sensitivity in the recognition of employees, these programs may have a negative effect on performance. For example, one HR manager at Siecor suggests that recognition programs can *de*motivate employees if recognition does not also reward the average performer for *improved* performance.

One of the most successful recognition programs operates at Siecor and was created by associates themselves. A team in one of the plants was responsible for the creation of an "Employee of the Month" program in which associates nominate their peers for recognition. A manager in the plant perceived that employees generally view this award as prestigious, where in other companies, "Employee of the Month" is more likely to be viewed as a popularity contest. It may be that recognition programs created and administered by employees are considered to be more meaningful, and less subject to favoritism by managers.

If recognition programs are to be considered fair by employees, then managers must consistently apply the programs. At Siecor, a few managers independently decided that certain aspects of the company recognition program were of minimal value (e.g., Employee of the Month). Subsequently, one department has this form of recognition, while another does not. Not only does the non-application of certain forms of recognition deviate from company-stated strategic policy, but it also provides an inconsistent message to employees as to what is valued behavior in the organization. Further, employees who see their peers recognized for performance, when they are not, may become demoralized, or disillusioned with the way company policies are put into practice. Although there can be positive benefits from tailoring recognition to meet group needs, variation in recognition programs within a company may have a negative impact on employees, who feel (despite what the manager thinks) that a particular form of recognition is worthwhile.

LESSONS LEARNED

In the areas of employee reward and recognition, no easy methods exist for the creation of an environment in which workers feel appreciated, and in turn desire to significantly contribute to the success of the venture. However, reward and recognition programs appear the most effective when they are meaningful and consistently applied. To the extent that recognition programs are aligned with the strategic orientation of the venture, employees have a clear idea of what is considered important toward contributing to the goals of the company. Ignoring these considerations, reward and recognition programs can have a demotivating effect on employees, and thus detract from the original intent of the programs.

Although there are many forms of reward and recognition offered to employees in the ventures, additional forms of reward incentives might include:

- compensation for managers that ties their performance to JV successes;
- financial incentives to encourage cooperation among different groups (e.g., joint R&D and production task teams);
- a greater emphasis on rewards and recognition for teams, especially when that is a strategic priority for the venture; and
- rewards and recognition for employees for improved performance.

CHAPTER 12

Performance Appraisal: A Necessary Component?

Not having a performance review system—that's a big problem, very big. Simply because you have people who are working hard, going the extra mile, doing their job and they're getting the same amount of money as a person here who is not doing their job, or just does enough to barely get by. So there's nothing that separates the two . . . even if you got some feedback from management [such as] "you've been doing a great job, thank you." Compared to the person who does not do their job. Just anything would be great. But you hear nothing.

Production Associate, Diamond Star

The goal of JV companies such as Mayo Forest Products, OCG, Siecor, and Diamond Star is to create conditions under which JV staff can excel in meeting the competitive demands of a global market. Performance reviews are one way to sensitize employees to performance objectives, provide them with performance feedback, and allow managers to gain a better appreciation of employee skills, difficulties, and career aspirations. Yet despite the possibility of obtaining critical information from the performance appraisal (PA) process, managers repeatedly said that employee reviews were a bother, and inconsistently done—if done at all. To some extent this was a function of time, but in many cases managers seemed to think the reviews were not of essential value. It may be that in companies where employees receive feedback from other sources (e.g., from supervisors on a regular basis), PA systems are not of primary importance.

A MATTER OF SPORADIC ATTENTION

Of all HRM activities, the area of performance review generally receives the least attention by JV managers. At Mayo Forest Products, essentially no performance appraisal process operates for either hourly or salaried staff. OCG has a "Performance Management Process" in operation which is a system adopted from the American parent. The purpose of this system is to link employee performance with the Total Quality program. Employee progress is monitored related to meeting customer expectations, and is based on both team and individual goals. Employees have input to the reviews, and technical as well as interpersonal skills are considered. There is a developmental component which focuses on career objectives or training requirements for employees. All employees at OCG receive a performance review, although the implementation is not consistent within the company.

At Siecor, performance reviews for salaried employees are based on a "Management-by-Objective" (MBO) system in which the employee and immediate supervisor jointly set performance goals. There is a developmental component, under which employee performance is reviewed related to requirements for future job fits in the company. Managers are given training in how to conduct appraisals, and guidelines exist for both managers and employees in order that the process is completed successfully. Hourly employees in the plants also receive performance reviews based on both work performance and personal traits; at the time of the review, employee objectives are set for the coming year. In the future, peer reviews for production associates are expected to operate in the plants. To ensure the completion of performance reviews for all staff, merit increases are only processed once the PA has been received by the personnel department.

A PA system exists at Diamond Star for salaried staff, but not for associates. The process focuses on the accomplishment of both performance goals and personal skills, and the PA is used primarily to determine salary increases. Considerable thought and preparation was devoted by HR staff in creating a PA system compatible with the requirements of Japanese managers in the plant. To facilitate the implementation of the performance reviews, training was provided to Japanese managers as to how to complete the process. Despite this, there are ongoing difficulties for the Japanese in the use of a system with which they are neither entirely comfortable nor familiar.

In all four joint ventures there is a strong emphasis on the value of production staff related to the creation of quality products in the venture. Consequently, tremendous effort is allocated to the training of hourly production employees. However, it is interesting that only at OCG and Siecor is a performance review process provided to hourly workers. Further, as one associate at Diamond Star comments, he would like to see a PA system in place in the plant in order that employees are better informed about their job performance. In this context, a performance review system is viewed as a chance to have better interaction with supervisors. In companies where feedback to employees about work performance is regularly provided, an institutionalized system for performance review may be less necessary. Otherwise, the PA may be the only way in which employees know how they are doing.

MEETING STRATEGIC OBJECTIVES

To meet strategic objectives, the PA system will ideally reinforce central operating requirements of the company such as quality, teamwork, or continuous improvement. Based on overall company objectives, employees are rewarded for the accomplishment of personal goals in each area. At OCG the Performance Management Process is a format in which company objectives of meeting customer requirements are individualized for employees. Performance is judged against various customer expectations. As the HR Manager points out, this system has the advantage of not relying on a single supervisor's evaluation and is based on multiple input.

To elaborate, employees at OCG meet with their supervisor and determine primary customers. Feedback is obtained from designated customers related to their current expectations, whether or not the expectations were met, and future requirements. Employees are not rated on a point system for performance, but rather on whether or not they meet customer expectations in relation to the determined objectives. The process allows supervisors to know about employee objectives for career advancement, or of additional training that may be required.

The Performance Management Process operates to differing degrees at OCG. Performance reviews are not returned to the HR Manager by supervisors, and subsequently it is difficult to determine who is completing the process, and to what level of effectiveness. One manager who is located at the headquarters office remarks that performance reviews tend to be more informal than formal. In his view, Performance Management is not used consistently, and he adds if the process is to be effectively implemented, a "top down" approach will be required which is tailored to the unique requirements of OCG.

The performance review system at Diamond Star likewise mirrors the strategic goals for the venture. Quality, teamwork, Kaizen, cost-consciousness, problem-solving, and other personal and technical skills are considered. Further, if company goals focus on the increase of technology exchange, or executive contributions to the joint venture, then these items should be important to the review process. Although performance reviews are traditionally for individuals, in companies where a team approach is predominant, managers may want to consider the application of "team reviews." In all of these cases, the PA system aims to match company strategic goals.

SIECOR: PERFORMANCE REVIEW IMPLEMENTED IN PRACTICE

A personnel manager at Siecor's corporate office comments that performance appraisal for salaried employees is done in order to have a record of an individual's performance over the year, and as a reference for future job fits. There is a developmental component under which additional skills an employee may require to move into another job are considered. The personnel manager adds that although this is his perspective on how appraisals should operate, others in the organization view the review process differently. Another executive remarks that the purpose of appraisals is to "try and find the stars" and to create opportunities for them in the long-term plan of the company. Alternately, appraisals are a way to separate out the "dead wood" and for repositioning or downgrading employees when necessary. For some managers, the most important reason for performance reviews is to determine if established objectives have been met, and subsequently the magnitude of salary increases. Although Siecor has tried to separate compensation from performance, the linkage remains.

Performance appraisal is done once a year by the immediate supervisor, and according to the personnel manager, supervisors actually complete the reviews. Managers are given training in how to complete appraisals, and the personnel manager mentions that performance appraisal is done much more frequently than it was four or five years ago. The personnel department ensures this, and "no merit increase will be processed unless there was a performance review submitted." Late submissions of reviews are tracked by the personnel group. The president of Siecor endorses the importance of the performance appraisal process, and consequently the personnel manager notes, "it's a rarity when someone gets their performance appraisal late."

Appraisals for exempt employees (e.g., managers, supervisors, and administrative/technical staff) are based on an MBO system. Performance for the year is matched to the previously set goals. Major accomplishments, strengths, developmental needs, training objectives, and career interests or plans of the employee are ideally considered.

Accompanying the performance review is a "Managerial/Individual Behavior Inventory" which lists various work-related behaviors. This form serves as a behavioral checklist for the supervisor and the employee during the performance review process, and can also be used as a guide to setting future performance goals. The form is completed separately by both the manager and employee, and then ratings on various items are jointly compared during the performance review. Items for consideration include commitment to quality (i.e., meeting customer requirements, product improvement, and problem-solving); commitment to people (i.e., communication skills, the ability to take initiative); and commitment to leadership (i.e., goal setting, creating a team atmosphere, and managing for results). Also, a guide is available to employees explaining how to prepare for the review and suggesting questions they might want to ask of the manager. It is recommended the review take two and a half hours.

Hourly employees in Siecor's plants also receive a performance evaluation in which both performance and personal traits are considered. Employee and supervisor determine objectives to be accomplished if the employee is to advance at the next salary rate. Employees are reviewed every two months for the first year relative to pay increases. After this period there is typically a six month and then a one year review. According to managers in both plants, the progression is automatic as long as the employee demonstrates adequate performance.

The plant HR Manager notes employee performance is tied to the pay scale, but "there are no measures, it's totally subjective." Some supervisors have developed their own performance measures for employees, although there is no consistency from one supervisor to another. Reviews are done by supervisors, and as with salaried staff the HR department does not process salary adjustments until the employee performance review is received. The aim in the plants is to eventually move toward a peer review process for all teams. In one experimental team where a peer review already has been tried, an associate remarks that the performance review is collectively done by team members, and the team leader sits in. Referring to the team leader role, the associate continues, "They [the team leaders] usually don't have any input, they just kind of sit back and listen to what we have to say. If something really gets out of hand that they may agree or disagree with, they'll put their two cents worth in." Otherwise, the review is left to the team members. The associate considers this to be a fair process, and adds the team members are in the best position to observe how an employee performs.

APPRAISAL CONSIDERATIONS IN AN AMERICAN-JAPANESE JOINT VENTURE

As already noted, Diamond Star has a PA system for salaried (e.g., managerial, supervisory, administrative) staff but not for associates. Appraisals are completed annually from February to April and are used to determine salary increases. The "Performance Planning and Review" form consists of a single, two-sided sheet of paper. On one side of the form performance goals are listed, and the accomplishment of those goals is recorded on a five-point scale. There is an optional section on this side of the page where an employee can state career interests and goals or developmental needs. The reverse side of the form lists 13 "methods/factors" which are also evaluated on a five-point scale. Items to be considered include quality, teamwork or "Wa" (harmony), Kaizen, cost-consciousness, planning, problem solving, leadership, communication, job knowledge, employee equal opportunity, support, interpersonal skills, safety awareness, and attendance. An information package accompanies the form in order to explain to managers the meaning of the various terms. In keeping with the management philosophy infused into Diamond Star from Mitsubishi, considerable emphasis is placed on interpersonal rather than technical skills. There is a focus on quality, effort dedicated to continuous improvement, and the maintenance of harmonious work relationships.

The format for employee evaluation was made deliberately short and simple in order that Japanese managers would be able to complete the form with a minimal amount of difficulty. Japanese managers were consulted regarding the format and content of the performance review sheet. An HR manager explains that originally the Japanese managers at Diamond Star did not want to do appraisals, and that in Japan an appraisal process does not exist. One Japanese manager notes that the Japanese at Diamond Star had "severe difficulty" with the idea of a review in which explicit feedback is given to an employee. He said, "Most of the Japanese managers are not accustomed to negotiation, and sometimes they were emotional. But now they are accustomed to this [PA] system and they know the points."

The current system of performance review was implemented in 1988. Prior to this time salary increases for employees were based primarily on length of service. A manager in the HR department comments about the process involved in assisting the Japanese in the completion of staff appraisals:

We developed a system, a program, that we thought was easy to understand. We spent some time in training. We answered their [Japanese managers] questions, and kind of forced them to do it. We told them this is the way it has to be done in the United States. So from that they were obviously very reluctant, didn't want to do it. We made some revisions to it [the review process]. We increased the training in the following year and now there doesn't seem to be much of a problem with it.

Despite the attempt to streamline the PA system, there remain some difficulties with the procedure. Diamond Star managers who remain employees of either Chrysler or Mitsubishi are appraised by their superior in the parent company if they have no superior at Diamond Star. In the case of Mitsubishi, the President or Executive Vice-Presidents at Diamond Star will provide parent company executives with information related to the performance of Japanese dispatchees at Diamond Star. Under the current system, managers at Diamond Star do the performance reviews of Diamond Star staff (i.e., who are neither Mitsubishi nor Chrysler employees) who report to them directly. There is a distinction, however: Japanese managers will be appraised only by other Japanese, but Americans can be appraised by Japanese managers. In the case of the Vice-President for Finance, for example, he does not evaluate Japanese managers who report to him directly. This is done by one of the Japanese Vice-Presidents.

Even given the responsibility to do appraisals, the Japanese are hesitant to be involved in the process. One senior Japanese manager mentions he prefers to have his American counterpart do his appraisals on other American managers, although he does the PA for Japanese managers who report to him. From an American manager's perspective, he notes the Japanese do not want to be put in the position of evaluating an American and telling them "how they should be as a person." One American manager who is appraised by a Japanese superior notes the Japanese "have a really rough time. They don't do that [PA] in Japan. And he hates it, he puts it off to the very last second. And they're [the appraisals] probably five minutes, if that. And he wants to get out as quick as he can." This branch manager adds his Japanese supervisor rates all the branch managers who report to him in the same way. Another American who is appraised by a Japanese manager states, "I just received my first performance appraisal from my manager in April and it was extremely good. But I wonder if he would actually criticize me, if you know what I mean. Or if he knows how to do it."

CREATING EFFECTIVE PA SYSTEMS

In order to meet the evolving needs of employees and the company, ideally a developmental component is part of the appraisal. This may include the designation of long-term and short-term career goals for employees, as well as related training requirements. When performance goals are fixed and inflexible, then there is little opportunity for employees to respond to changing contingencies in the company. For example, in fast-moving entrepreneurial firms with global associations, a flexible PA process is more likely to fit employee and company requirements than one in which performance goals and expectations are static.

Further, performance appraisal may be more meaningful to employees if goals are not unilaterally determined by supervisors, but involve joint input from employees in which they can "buy into the process." This form of PA would be most consistent with the goals of companies that aim to provide high levels of responsibility and involvement to employees. Siecor is one example where employee involvement is evolving in the area of PA, where associates conduct "peer reviews" of one another.

PA will operate most effectively if it is consistently applied. At Siecor and Diamond Star, the HR departments offered training in the PA process to managers and others responsible for appraisals. In addition, written materials are made available to both managers and employees in order that they have a better understanding of the procedure. This helps to ensure that managers and supervisors understand the PA system, and know how it is to be applied.

In joint ventures, a further issue is whether the PA process will be based on the PA systems operating in one of the parent firms, or developed to suit the specific needs of the venture. As in other HR policy areas, there may be a time and cost savings if the PA system is adapted from the parent firms. The trade-off is that the appraisal system may not exactly match the objectives of the venture.

When diverse national cultures are represented, the creation of a PA system appropriate to all groups is likely to pose unique challenges. For example, at Diamond Star the HR staff took great pains to create a simple PA system, with input from Japanese managers. Values and operating preferences of each cultural group were considered related to the development of a culturally-sensitive PA format. To assist the Japanese in the application of PA procedures, the HR department developed appraisal training programs.

LESSONS LEARNED

Of all HR areas, the performance review process receives the least attention and is the most inconsistent. However, there are some lessons to consider based on the experiences of companies where performance appraisals operate effectively. They include:

• to meet strategic company objectives, the PA system will be structured to reinforce key norms and operation requirements (e.g., for teamwork or continuous improvement);

• for PA to be implemented consistently, it will require support from senior managers as well as mid-level managers, supervisors, and other employees;

• in companies where a team approach is predominant, managers may want to consider "team reviews";

• to ensure the reviews are completed, the HR group may wish to consider tracking review submissions;

• in companies where diverse cultural groups are present, PA forms are most acceptable if they are short and simple, and based on input from members of each culture;

- training assists to ensure that the PA process is understood by staff members responsible for completing the reviews, and helps to provide consistency in the review process.

PART IV

Special Issues

CHAPTER 13

Richness and Complexity when Diverse National Cultures Combine

> Probably the biggest thing in terms of joint ventures, or I should say working with the Japanese, or with any other culture, is the fear—the uncertainty of the other culture.... There's more emotion involved in coming to work here everyday in a joint venture environment between foreign companies, and working for a foreign company in your own country.... It's been difficult. I think it's harder if you're a person that likes direction and continuity ... it's always changing here.
>
> Supervisor, Diamond Star

International joint ventures between culturally diverse partners offer unique opportunities for learning at the organizational level. The partners may potentially gain information and skills related to each other's management practices or culture. In the realm of HRM, new policies and practices can be created in a way that match the needs and requirements of JV groups. Alternately, culturally diverse joint ventures can pose overwhelming challenges to managers who fail to embrace a philosophy of synergy rising from diversity. For many employees, cultural diversity compounded by language difficulties is threatening. There is less certainty about how work is to be accomplished.

The challenges and outcomes in each joint venture are particular to the company's strategy, culture, and people. However, Diamond Star represents a good example of how members of the HR department, along with other managers in the plant, endeavoured to create culturally appropriate HR policy and practice that meshed Japanese philosophy and production techniques with the expectations of the largely American workforce. The impetus behind the changes and the process for the creation of new policies is elaborated in this chapter. Further, American employees at DSM share their opinions about working in an environment where culturally diverse parents both have an active presence.

THE RELATIVE IMPACT OF CULTURE IN JOINT VENTURE FIRMS

Despite that Mayo Forest Products, OCG, Siecor, and Diamond Star are all the product of a union between international partners, only at Diamond Star is national culture a significant concern related to the development of culturally sensitive HRM policy and practice. At Mayo, OCG, and Siecor (where there are few or no expatriates who do not speak English), HRM policy either parallels policies in the American or Canadian parent firms, or was created for the joint venture with little need for cultural adaptation. Alternately, at Diamond Star both American and Japanese managers are actively involved in the venture, and new HR policy is created which draws on the preferences of Japanese managers adapted to the largely American work group.

Cultural differences are represented in "shades of gray" rather than in absolute terms. Perceptions of culture by members within a given joint venture vary. An interesting finding at Diamond Star is the fact that some Japanese managers, as well as some of the American managers, do not view their respective cultures as widely divergent. These managers generally prefer to consider that both similarities and differences exist between the national cultures of the United States and Japan. Other managers continue to maintain that the cultural divide is huge.

Further, Mitsubishi managers at DSM note that generalizing management practices as being Japanese is false, and that commonalties exist between Japanese and American management styles, or between Japanese and American managers and workers. To elaborate, a Japanese Vice-President at Diamond Star comments,

I don't really know what is the Japanese management system that many people talk about, you know. Some people may say that it's lifetime employment, or consensus management, but it is not new or unique to Japan. It is also in America. In Japan, lifetime employment is not necessarily so.

Related to these remarks, it is possible that many of the accepted concepts of what comprises Japanese work orientations or practices may be overstated. For example, a Japanese and an American manager who work together at Diamond Star both suggest some differences between the cultures of the two groups have been exaggerated. In the area of planning, for instance, a Japanese manager remarks that although the Japanese as a whole are considered to be good long-term planners, Americans also excel at long-range planning, and alternately some Japanese do not.

In addition, a senior Japanese manager at Diamond Star comments it is false for Americans to assume Japanese employees work primarily for the intrinsic satisfaction of accomplishing a job. He adds that in Japan employees work hard because they are actually striving for better jobs or salaries. However, because time frames for accomplishing goals are longer, employee motivations may not be transparent to an external observer. This same manager suggests that although there is a collective or "group" philosophy that operates *to some extent* in Japan, there is also considerable emphasis on the individual and individually-oriented criteria. He stresses that to motivate employees (either in Japan, or when working with Japanese employees outside Japan), managers often offer individual encouragement. In his view, a distinction operates: in Japan a "group philosophy" applies when employees consider their allegiance to the company; however, the treatment of employees is on a more individual basis.

As a further example, a Japanese manager explains that contrary to popular belief, Japanese do not avoid conflict at all costs. On a subtle level, much depends on the *context* in which these discussions occur. Open discussion with one's boss occurs in certain circumstances, but conflicts are likely to be avoided when "outsiders" are present. Related to the importance of context, previous research has considered the relative determinants of conflict management in United States/Japanese joint ventures (Mendenhall and Black, 1990). More specifically, depending on the organizational or social situation, the *appearance* of harmony is more important than the actual absence of conflict. Context determines interpretation.

THE CULTURAL CHALLENGE

Within the organizational framework of Diamond Star, Japanese and American managers work together to create an efficient manufacturing operation staffed by primarily American workers. Different styles of operation and philosophical variations prevail among the groups represented at Diamond Star. There is a conscious attempt by Diamond Star management to blend the cultures of the two national groups into policies and processes that are appropriate for a company which seeks to manufacture automobiles in a way previously unfamiliar to most of the American auto industry. On a personal level, managers at the plant need to communicate to each other, despite language difficulties. The nuances of what each group wants to accomplish, and why, are not always easily comprehensible.

A Japanese executive in the HRM area points out the importance of being able to merge the Japanese and American cultures. He suggests this requires a great deal of trust and flexibility from all concerned. The management philosophies prevalent at Mitsubishi cannot be introduced to the

North American plant without modification. However, creating suitable policy for Diamond Star is a challenge. He continues it is "very difficult to find out what is adequate, what is not adequate. Still we are struggling." Another Japanese manager explains, "if we can say that both cultures completely mixed is 100 percent, we are now 45 or 50 percent of the way [at Diamond Star]." He adds that in every meeting the managers at Diamond Star face cultural issues. From an American manager's perspective, he notes that when ideas are presented the Americans and the Japanese see things very differently. Both groups often become frustrated by approaches embedded in diverse operating styles. "It's not necessarily that either person is opposed to the other's idea. The objective that they're trying to accomplish is probably mutual. But the road that they want to take is totally different."

A Japanese executive comments that differences between the American and Japanese points of view go beyond a comparison of "so-called Japanese management style" versus American practices. On a deeper level the executive remarks,

The base culture [of the United States and Japan] is completely different, so we think it takes time to understand each other. . . . It's very easy to simplify the different philosophies between the Japanese and the American companies such as no layoffs, or training within the company or promotion within the company, or so-called lifetime employment. But it is very superficial.

The Japanese executive observes that many of the difficulties they experience at Diamond Star are related to differences in expectations between American and Japanese employees. In the area of promotion, for example, career advancement is much slower in Japan because of longer time-lines for employment with the company. He adds American workers don't understand this arrangement, and are impatient for fast promotions. In another area, the Japanese executive notes most of the Japanese managers are frustrated because they are not able to hire manufacturing engineers in the United States with broad-based skills. He adds that in the United States, employees are too specialized in their job experience and knowledge, as opposed to Japan where a wide range of skills is valued. Consequently, how to train and hire is different in Japan.

In the area of job rotation, a representative of Mitsubishi comments that generally people expect job rotation in Japanese companies, but from a practical point of view job rotation is desirable only when employees have extensive knowledge of a particular job. In Japan, a worker who has been in a job for five years is still considered "green." Therefore, it may take five years or longer for a worker to be rotated to another position in a Japanese factory. Time perspectives are longer related to a worker's expectation of being with a single company for an extended period of time. In contrast, employees at Diamond Star may expect to be rotated to different positions after relatively short time-frames, after attaining only partial job skill knowledge. Some of the Japanese managers find these expectations unrealistic.

The meaning of work and the form of work relations differ in some important aspects between American and Japanese workers. One Japanese manager points out that contrary to popular opinion, Japanese managers have "business fights" with each other and do not necessarily strive to avoid conflicts. This is the case in the relationship he shares with his boss, although he adds this does not imply a lack of respect. Citing an example, the Japanese manager remarks he will usually ask permission of his boss to leave the office in the evening, or ask if he might still be needed. He does this because he and his boss are "sharing the business" together. He suggests there is a difference between Japanese and Americans related to mutual work relationships. Japanese employees feel they are "sharing life" with their coworkers. "[The] job is a part of the life to Japanese . . . but to Americans . . . it's kind of an assignment maybe, a contract with each other. . . . There is a difference."

BRIDGING CROSS-CULTURAL DIFFERENCES

Sensitivity to another individual's operating style is imperative. One manager describes the biggest challenge for employees at Diamond Star is to try and understand the cultural differences, and how these differences influence management styles and decisions. A manager sums this sentiment in the following way, "Both sides of the culture in terms of management [e.g., Japanese and American]—there has to be much more awareness of the counterpart in terms of cultural sensitivity, the understanding and also the willingness to change on both sides." Cross-cultural training can assist in the process. In addition, there need to be qualified staff who are able to operate in a "bicultural setting."

In the General Affairs Department at Diamond Star (the Japanese analogue to Administrative Services in the United States), there are two managers who have bicultural skills. In different ways these individuals are able to operate in the role of cultural interpreter or liaison between the Japanese and Americans at Diamond Star. For example, one female manager is completely fluent in both Japanese and English, and has long-term experience living in both Japan and the United States. In the past she has been able to provide vital links related to language and cultural explanations. In this capacity, she was involved in the union-management negotiations at Diamond Star. This individual remarks that Japanese managers are more likely to come to her for advice than are the American managers.

The other bicultural manager in the General Affairs Department has served as a liaison for the Japanese who are on temporary assignment at Diamond Star. He describes himself as a "buffer" between Americans and Japanese. This manager arranged for accommodation, schools, and other services for the technical people transferred from Mitsubishi to Diamond Star. He is a link to the community and gives presentations to local groups related to the Japanese presence in the area. In addition, this individual arranges for visits to Diamond Star, a large task considering that in a single year there can be as many as 2,000 visitors to the plant.

It has been a difficult task for the management of Diamond Star to create an integrated corporate culture. Each parent firm brings diverse philosophies and operating styles to the venture. These philosophies and styles tend to be influenced by the norms and values represented in the national society to which each of these parent firms belong. In the case of Japan and the United States, there are some operating similarities, but also many differences related to how work policies ought to be enacted. For example, in the Human Resources area, one American manager discusses the difficulty he has in creating HR policy which executives of both parent companies can accept. He says this process is frustrating "because there are two different philosophies," and both the Americans and the Japanese support their corporate cultures for how Diamond Star should operate. He adds philosophical divergence between the parent firms has made it difficult for managers at Diamond Star to determine a unique culture and identity for the venture, a culture separate from each of the parent firms. This sentiment is reflected by a Japanese manager at Diamond Star, who explains that for the first five years there has been a strong influence from Mitsubishi, and now most employees at Diamond Star understand Japanese business styles, Japanese thought, and Japanese production methods. Over time, however, he emphasized the importance of determining Diamond Star's "own way."

THE DEVELOPMENT OF "HYBRID" HR POLICY

HR policy is created for Diamond Star that consciously draws from both American and Japanese management practice. One senior Japanese manager comments on the need to form a "hybrid" system of HR policy and practice. Consideration is given to the fact the majority of the associates in the plant are American. An HR manager notes,

When you've got multinational involvement, whatever country you're going to have your plant in, wherever you're going to stock your plant, the customs, traditions, behavior patterns of that country have to be accepted. . . . There is a lot of similarity actually between Japanese and American workers. There are probably more similarities than dissimilarities, but the dissimilarities are striking. And while you can shape your work environment, shape your corporate philosophy and your corporate culture a certain way, there are just limits on what you can do. So part of HR is to know what the limits are and to make sure that the management understands them.

Related to this, part of the task for HR managers is the creation of policy appropriate for employees, while at the same time taking the goals and the norms of both parent companies into consideration. The individual cited above adds that at the upper management level at Diamond Star, all managers should be informed as to what is accepted policy in the United States. This may include legislation related to hiring and firing practices, or workman's compensation, among other things.

In order to create a blend of HR policy and practice, both American and Japanese managers in the HR area have worked together from the conception of Diamond Star to try and understand each other's HR orientations. In the first years of the joint venture, both the American HR General Manager and the Japanese HR Assistant General Manager traveled to Japan several times a year to allow the American manager to get better acquainted with HRM policy at Mitsubishi. Many of the managers at Diamond Star are Japanese and provide their insights as to appropriate HR practice on an ongoing basis. In addition, the HR Assistant General Manager (who is Japanese) mentions that to gain greater knowledge of American personnel practices, he had at one time worked with a colleague in the HR department at Chrysler. Some policies were largely adapted from Chrysler, such as the health insurance plan. One manager notes creating linkages with the American parent firm is beneficial in order to have access to certain HR policy information. The Personnel Administration Manager at Diamond Star had at one time been a Chrysler employee. When he left the company in 1989, the direct link from HR at Diamond Star and HR at Chrysler was severed.

To get broad managerial input to new HR policies, staff in the HR department typically draft a policy and then distribute it for review prior to implementation to Chrysler, Mitsubishi, and Diamond Star managers who work on the DSM plant site. According to one manager, this is done in order that all groups totally understand the policy, and are able to provide their comments. The HR Assistant General Manager will often act in the role of cultural interpreter, in order to explain the rationale behind a particular policy to other Japanese managers. According to various HR managers, a policy may be rewritten many times, making this a very time-consuming process. In some instances, when major policy changes are involved, the Executive Vice-President for HR will take the policy to the Board of Directors for approval.

EMPLOYEE OPINIONS OF WORKING IN AN AMERICAN-JAPANESE JOINT VENTURE

There are clearly demarcated views held by Diamond Star employees about the two parent companies, each who have a presence in the plant. Although not a generalization of all Diamond Star staff (who are mostly American), there is a clear preference by most employees who participated in this study for the Japanese-influenced methods of management, and very little enthusiasm for the participation of Chrysler at Diamond Star. One manager at Diamond Star who is a Chrysler employee describes this situation in the following way:

When I first came here [to Diamond Star] there was a tremendous resentment for Chrysler. The Japanese were the heroes. They provided this plant. Chrysler put up half of it, but the Japanese were given the authority to manage and run it in the agreement. So there was a tremendous resentment about American Chrysler people being here. . . . A lot [of Chrysler managers] have left and a lot are guilty of not doing anything when they were here. They took it as a free ride. Some of us didn't, and we made an earnest effort to help and got involved.

When difficulties exist between the Japanese and American parent firms, awareness of the problems filters well beyond the management ranks to associates. One associate comments,

You have the Japanese management on one side, the Chrysler management on the other, and they don't communicate and so what comes down to you are two different views of the same thing. I like the Japanese philosophy because I enjoy working hard and I get excited about being able to accomplish something. And the American management is, well, do what you can. It's not as, I want to say hardnosed, as the Japanese way of life. The Japanese expect you to do a good job. And you don't have that same expectation with the American managers. They seem to manage through threats. Where the Japanese seem to say, "this is your job. It needs to be done."

This associate elaborates that the Japanese on the floor are well liked and respected. In contrast, he mentions the Chrysler managers are

Snobbish, arrogant, they won't come down and talk to anybody. If you say "hi" to them, it's just, they keep on walking. Where the Japanese managers will stand and talk to you. Even the President when he was on the floor, he'll stop and talk to everybody. You don't have the same with the Chrysler management.

In his view, he thinks:

Chrysler managers tend to blame everything on the Japanese management. . . . If you can't get a straight answer it's blamed on the people who weren't there, which is normally the Japanese management. . . . One thing I would love to see is if the Japanese take completely over. Because I like their management style a lot better than the American or Chrysler style of management.

Two American managers who have previously worked in automotive factories in the United States both remark there is greater respect for the individual in the Diamond Star plant than at other plants where they have been employed. One manager notes,

While I don't always know what's going on, I'd have to say that I've been treated better here in the last four years than I've ever been treated any other place I've worked, in terms of respect for the way you're treated. . . . I would never have this opportunity anyplace else, I've learned more in four years than I did in all the other years I worked anyplace else. I probably learned twice as much.

Another American manager with previous auto plant experience also likes to work at Diamond Star. He observes, "it's a good place to work," adding the Japanese and the American workers get along. There are "no yelling contests," where in other auto plants "it was how well you could demean somebody." He said at Diamond Star people do not raise their voices. At other plants, he remarks, "everyday you'd wonder how many battles you were going to get into at the plant. Well, here you don't get into any."

One other element employees seem to like about Diamond Star is the sense of equality derived from all staff wearing uniforms, from the President to associates. An American manager observes Diamond Star is not a strong union plant and with respect to this he states,

You know what I think makes a lot of difference to all of that [i.e., regarding union support]—this uniform, the breakdown in how you're perceived in the shop. The fact that my engineers are out there right now, and if we walked out on the floor you wouldn't be able to tell the manager of production from a guy on the floor. And in all my years of working with a tie and out on the floor, you might as well walk around with a sign on your head, "I'm better than you. I'm management. You're nothing." And you know, believe it or not I think the uniforms make a big, big difference. Everybody's the same.

LESSONS LEARNED

The managers in this study note that although in some cases the cultural differences are striking, in many instances culture is represented in "shades of gray." Employees further point out that generalizing management practices as being Japanese is too simplistic. In turn, this remark suggests that closer attention be paid to the *context* of the situation in which action occurs.

Sensitivity to differences in operating styles that result from culture is imperative, and cross-cultural training can assist in the acculturation process. Despite this, cultural training had been phased out at Diamond Star, and was not a focus in the other ventures in this investigation. Managers may want to consider the merits of both cultural training and hiring staff with bicultural skills to mediate across cultures.

In the establishment of HR policy and practice to accommodate diverse cultures, the HR group is advised to (1) consult with a range of managers from different cultural groups prior to policy formation and (2) solicit the assistance of a "cultural interpreter" in this process who can explain foreign aspects of a policy.

CHAPTER 14

From a Planned to a Market Economy: The Case of Central and Eastern Europe

The issue is that the people [Czechs] have to adjust themselves to a free and democratic society—that they are no longer under strict regulations that . . . they were forced to take as a system of life. And they lived with it and now they are free, and they are looking for new values to replace the old regulations, and this is not so easy.

German expatriate in a German-Czech joint venture

The rate of organizational change in joint ventures between Western European companies and Central/Eastern European companies located in Poland, Hungary and the Czech Republic is nothing short of phenomenal. Local managers and employees are generally well educated and eager to learn new managerial and technical skills. The Western partner is interested in expanding into Eastern markets, and consequently is willing to invest capital and technology in the venture. Local staff are watching carefully to see if the Western investor intends a long-term commitment to the joint venture, rather than viewing the venture as an opportunity to make "quick money" and leave.

The levers of change in East/West joint ventures are complex. Important issues include how management responsibility is shared between the partner firms, how attitudes influenced by the Communist legacy might be changed, and how staffing, training, and reward systems can be creatively implemented to meet the JV strategic initiatives.[1]

SHARING MANAGEMENT RESPONSIBILITY

Development of a "partnership" between local and foreign managers that fosters trust and mutual respect is important. The involvement of local managers in the creation of new strategies, structures, and practices allows the joint ventures to benefit from the strengths of both partners. Ideally, not only are local managers willing to accept additional responsibilities, but foreign managers are open to learning about local practices that worked well in the past.

Local managers are proud, and want to prove they can both adapt to new ways, as well as offer unique contributions to the venture. A Czech manager in a German-Czech joint venture remarks, "We want to show the Germans that we are as good." Mutual respect is critical. In one joint venture, the local employees mention they sometimes feel they are treated like "natives just down from the trees." As local employees gain competence through training, coaching, and teamwork, foreign managers are more likely to give them additional responsibility.

In a German-Czech joint venture, local and foreign managers are paired in an effort to exchange management and technical information. Although in theory this staffing arrangement is a way to transfer "know-how" into the venture, in reality the success of this practice depends on foreign managers who are willing to share responsibility and take a long-term view of what could be accomplished in the venture. In turn, local employees must be willing to embrace change and accept additional responsibilities. Two pitfalls to learning are identified as (1) trying to balance short-term success with long-term development and (2) matching employee expectations with what could realistically be achieved considering the large-scale transformation required in the venture. Finding middle ground between the methods and practices in use by the foreign partner, and developing new policies to match the unique requirements of the joint venture poses a significant challenge. A German manager remarks,

It is difficult to synchronize the procedures. The experts, they come from a very big enterprise and they have certain procedures, and rules, and regulations which are proper for a big enterprise. . . . And they transfer their procedures, their regulations, their behaviors, attitudes to this company. In some cases, this causes conflict.

The imposition of the foreign partner's values or operating procedures has the result of stifling innovation and reducing employee motivation. A senior manager in an Austrian-Hungarian joint venture in Hungary suggests local employees will excel if given the opportunity. He notes,

Hungarians are creative, proud, difficult to accept the ideas of others, but if we understand what they [Austrians] are thinking, then we are able to do better. But Austrians don't believe we can do as well as they. Austrians come and say they know better. They don't believe.

A CULTURAL DIMENSION

In the wake of the Communist system in Poland, Hungary, and the Czech Republic, culture has significance on at least two important dimensions. First, learning is needed to adjust for national/post-Communist ideology which discouraged risk-taking, quality performance, or competitiveness. Cultural understanding on the part of foreign managers of local culture and ideologies is important. Second, a new corporate culture needs to be woven for the venture—a culture that has relevance to the values and requirements of the locals, while at the same time is consistent with foreign policy and practice for the accomplishment of specific company strategic objectives.

To elaborate, learning at the organizational level requires a shift in work values and philosophy. A German manager in the German-Czech joint venture remarks,

The most difficult task is to train the people, to see their own responsibility, because many of the people claim that there are things going wrong beyond their own responsibility. But now they [Czechs] need to learn they are responsible for the work they are doing, and for the job they have, and for certain results.

More specifically, based on the implementation of new systems in a French-Polish joint venture, some of the levers of change include:

- creating results-oriented structures and systems
- an emphasis on quality
- goal setting and feedback to employees
- encouraging employees to accept responsibility
- development of new reporting systems
- creating new financial, reward, and training systems

At the French-Polish joint venture, the Managing Director recognizes the need to better understand Polish attitudes, values, and expectations prior to the implementation of large-scale change. To achieve a better level of understanding, a consultant was hired to conduct a survey of employee expectations for the venture.

Further, an organizational culture would need to be created that signals to local employees that a new form of enterprise can be initiated. A key to this process is a clear definition of responsibilities and objectives in order that employees know what is required. In some cases, change is clouded by a lack of common understanding of market-oriented systems or the corporate strategy intended for the venture. Local employees and expatriates may not always have the same perceptions or expectations of the joint venture. One French manager in the French-Polish joint venture comments,

We want to turn the minds of people and to show them that working with a French company is possible. Working with French people is possible. Winning in some subjects is possible, and for that it was compulsory to . . . explain the strategy . . . just to make people a bit more positive or optimistic, seeing the operation starting again.

From the Hungarian perspective, a factory manager in the same joint venture says,

There were a lot of problems at the beginning because the French and Hungarians couldn't understand each other. Problems were not from language, but from education, technical [experience], and measurement systems. Slowly things are getting better. The thinking was totally different. Before we had almost no contact with the French and the French had no information about Hungary. The French knew nothing about Hungarian history.

Clear communication of goals, long-term and short-term strategy, and policies is central to the change process. However, communication is often impeded by poor reporting systems and a need for expediency over efficiency, or when managers hoard information as one way to retain power. Communication difficulties due to language differences exist, but are not as problematic as expected. In part this was due to a desire by local managers and employees to learn a foreign language.

A PROCESS FOR CREATING ORGANIZATIONAL CHANGE

A topic close to the hearts of joint venture managers is how can change most effectively evolve. The French General Manager in the French-Hungarian joint venture believes much has already changed, and thinks more problems have been solved in the first two years of the joint venture than in the 15 years before, when the factory was state-owned. A Hungarian manager in the same joint venture countered that in factories where there are no foreigners, similar changes are occurring. Others feel changes are not happening fast enough, and that factories should be modernized more rapidly with the aid of foreign investment.

Change has two primary dimensions. First and most important is attitudinal change. The second area of change is related to equipment and technology. Concerning the latter, workers in the French-Hungarian joint venture indicate they would request tools or equipment only to be told there was not sufficient funding. Obtaining spare parts (e.g., for older machinery) poses a particular problem. In general, most workers feel new machinery in the factories is required in order to enhance efficiency. A

Hungarian adds they will never be able to change and match Western requirements without the necessary resources. By way of illustration he provides an example: "If I have a cousin in the U.S. and she tells me what to cook, I can do it, but only if I am able to buy the correct ingredients here."

Related to changing the attitudes of the people, one Hungarian manager in the French-Hungarian joint venture muses that maybe there are too many challenges in too many areas. Another manager suggests it will be the next generation of managers who will have new ideas and knowledge for change. He states,

Since the changes, managers are unable to quickly change what they've done [in Hungary] for 30 years. For 30 years, we've been told what to do. Now we're told to do things and we don't do them because we don't know how, or we're too scared. Therefore, we need a new generation to reach general management.

As change in the factories is set to unfold, another major concern of workers is unemployment. Staff reductions in the French-Hungarian joint venture were begun by Hungarian managers prior to the JV formation. Workers were reduced 50 percent before the venture began in 1991, and by an additional 30 percent following the JV start-up. In response to fear of being laid off, a manager notes,

Everybody is a little scared because of unemployment. Because of this fear, workers do their job and don't say anything. And now there is almost no trade union to stand on the side of the workers.

Caution in action is important. One Hungarian General Manager illustrates: "There are the cows and the electrical shepherd. And the cows learn when to go close, and when to stay away from it [the electric current]."

UNIQUE AND STRATEGIC INITIATIVES

Although many of the change initiatives are orchestrated through Western partner managers, there are exceptions. In an interesting case of an Austrian-Hungarian joint venture in Hungary, the JV General Manager has taken steps to implement strategy and norms in the venture to compete in the local markets. The General Manager aims to make the venture the premier supplier of roof tiles in the Hungarian marketplace. He states that his strategy of placing the customer first began at a time when "this kind of thinking was not natural." Describing the progress in the venture, he remarks,

Perhaps success lies in these things. Our system changed in thinking and we began six years earlier than other companies. It is not simple. People can understand and have a positive attitude because they can hear another motto. And they are surprised how such things can occur here in Hungary. Of course, there were mistakes.

The General Manager's adoption of a quality and customer-oriented focus might be partially explained by his broad and international experience. He trained at the technical university as an electrician, also playing on the basketball team. Due to his sports involvement he had the opportunity to travel to France, Germany, Italy, and Austria. When he joined the joint venture in 1984 at the JV start-up, the General Manager made a conscious decision to create a new direction through identified strategic initiatives. He planned to (1) reduce hierarchical levels in the organization and implement more of a team approach, and (2) emphasize training.

To realize strategic objectives in the Austrian-Hungarian JV, employees are encouraged to use their own ideas and to operate more independently. There is a union in the plant but union support is weak. Employees work in informal "teams," and although the General Manager notes he has the final decision, employees have considerable autonomy. The General Manager describes the operation of the company as a "smooth hierarchy" in which staff are empowered to do things themselves. He illustrates his role using the following example:

In an orchestra there are musicians and head musicians and they can play alone without the conductor. I am the conductor. It is enough for the conductor to sometimes say there is something missing, but the orchestra can only play well when they are allowed.

The General Manager continues that at first it was difficult for workers to accept a system of greater worker independence. He adds,

They [the workers] are glad to make the changes and people would like to realize themselves. If you order or demand, they don't like it. Then you need a closed hierarchy. And if mistakes are not allowed, they say it was the other [who made the mistake]. If mistakes are O.K. then they learn from the mistakes and do better the next time. There were some small problems in creating this change, and there were some people who couldn't understand. But the majority understand. Workers don't think about this, but they understand the philosophy.

When asked about where his own philosophy was derived, the General Manager says he got these ideas from playing basketball. "Everyone needs to decide once in his life how groups can best play to be successful and win. And then it's very simple. I need the support of others." Concerning his own performance, he contrasts the old system of government orders with the current system in which profit and competitiveness are key words. Returning to the sports analogy, the General Manager remarks,

I am now in training myself to spring to a high height. Before I only jumped to a smaller height. Before I jumped 120 centimeters, now it's 130 centimeters. In the West, they are jumping 200 centimeters. We would like to be in the world championships. Before we were told 120 centimeters was enough. Now they [the workers] need to train themselves. And they want to be the world champions.

STAFFING THE VENTURES

In a manner that parallels the North American joint ventures identified in this book, in the ventures in Central/Eastern Europe employees at all levels are selected with broad skills. Ideally, expatriate managers have a knowledge of the local culture, multiple language skills, and international management experience. For instance, the members of the senior management team in the French-Polish joint venture were selected by the Managing Director based on their technical skills and multicultural backgrounds. Several managers were of Polish origin and were able to speak Polish. In addition, the management team had extensive international experience.

Other employees in the French-Polish joint venture were selected for positions based on technical skills and, importantly, on personal skills and language capabilities. Having a good attitude toward work is considered to be essential. The supervisor for recruitment and career development notes that candidates are desirable when they are:

* young
* hardworking (having in the past worked in a factory, as well as had extra jobs or their own business)
* enthusiastic, good communicators, and have a "quality of smile"
* active and not afraid to take risks
* willing to solve problems and improvise
* interested in continuous learning (e.g., have computer skills)
* able to speak multiple languages, with an emphasis on English.

TRAINING TO BE A "LEARNING COMPANY"

Training is a primary focus in all the ventures. Learning is generated by (1) a broad scope of training topics in both technical and personal areas and (2) the allocation of sufficient personnel and financial resources. The strategic intent on the part of the foreign partner is to prepare local employees in order that they can eventually operate the venture with minimal intervention from the foreign partner. As a Polish supervisor in the French-Polish joint venture comments, training is a way of "preparing the people to develop themselves."

Training across the joint ventures encompasses a wide range of areas such as: technical skills, management capabilities (delegation, leadership, teamwork, competitiveness), personal skills (communication, conflict resolution), and foreign languages. Training is provided on-site as well as at the foreign partner's facilities.

Of particular importance is training and development of middle managers. As described in a company report at the French-Polish joint venture:

Middle management is the key population in the action plan of transforming the company. Very heterogeneous, composed of engineers and supervisors, it has been considered as the most affected by the previous system. Misunderstood, often reduced to simple tasks, middle management needs to discover its true role in the working of the company. It will have to acquire a new behavior which lies somewhere between a relaxed style and a temptation to lead through authority.

Training programs for mid-level managers emphasize:

- principles in a market economy—markets, competition, profit, investment, quality standards, labor legislation;
- the social and economic transformation of the Polish firm, the electronic industry in Poland and the world, the strategy and positioning of the French parent firm;
- policies and organization of the joint venture;
- the role of middle management and the "new company management style";
- communication and teamwork;
- interpersonal relations in a work context;
- conflict resolution; and
- definition of objectives, problem-solving.

Although intentions are good, in some cases the barrage of training is overwhelming, and some local managers do not understand the underlying intent. In one joint venture, mid-level managers respond that the training was "interesting but how can I apply it to the job?" Creating a clear linkage between training and performance is therefore a prerequisite to the learning process.

Based on a commitment to training the people, the foreign partners in the joint ventures described here are willing to contribute substantial investments of both time and funds. For instance, in the first three months of the French-Polish joint venture, 2,000 days of technically-oriented training were provided. In the first year of operation of the German-Czech joint venture, almost 5,000 employees received some form of training. By the second year of that joint venture, the German partner had invested five million German Marks in training programs, and the training department had expanded from eight trainers in 1991 to 60 trainers in 1993.

REVISING THE REWARD SYSTEM

The development of new reward systems is instrumental in signaling to employees what behavior is valued in the new organizational system. In all the joint ventures described herein, a similar reward structure exists for local employees—one in which there is a fixed portion of the salary and a variable portion (usually about 20 percent) for performance factors such as quality, productivity, and attendance. A percentage of the variable portion of the salary can be withheld for non-performance in a certain area. However, in many instances, managers give all workers the same salary. This situation is either a hold-over from the previous "collective" system, or is an attempt to avoid jeopardizing the employee's employment security in economies where good jobs are very scarce. In this sense, the reward system provides either a negative incentive or no incentive for workers—with no established link between reward and performance.

More specifically, to motivate employees to perform to a high level in the French-Polish joint venture, a reward structure was created in which the variable portion of the salary is 20 percent for production workers and 30 percent for specialists and managers (excluding expatriates). Expatriates have individually negotiated contracts, with a one month annual bonus available for achieving targets. As in the French system, salary scales for different jobs are kept secret. The average salary of 800 French Francs per month (2 million zlotys or U.S. $160 per month) is considered good in the local market. The variable portion, or "incentive" can be lost based upon absenteeism, quality, and performance. For example, two days of illness could result in a five percent cut in pay; nine days illness could result in a 10 percent cut. This reward format was seen to penalize women in particular, who were more often absent due to family responsibilities. Senior management at the French-Polish joint venture argue that in principle, the reward system should provide incentives to workers, if applied properly. To obtain the full salary amount employees are judged by their supervisors on quality (achievement by the individual or group); productivity; attendance; and attitude toward their duties. Attitude toward work refers to the following criteria: discipline, availability, reliability, and responsibility for tasks; attitude toward others (friendliness, the ability to cooperate and communicate); appearance; initiative; and carefulness in improving professional skills. However, some employees were concerned that the system was still too subjective, relying completely on the super-visor's judgment.

"Real" or additional incentives were not provided for exemplary work. Employees indicate they are strongly in favor of a bonus system, and in fact the implementation of such a system may increase motivation to per-form at more competitive levels. Although rewards are important to all workers, other forms of motivation are also relevant in the Central/East-ern European context. In the Hungarian-Swedish joint venture, a rather surprising finding is that in a study conducted by the Swedish partner of what is important to Hungarian workers, salary ranked in only 8th to 9th place. Instead, job satisfaction was linked to the work place situation, train-ing opportunities, job rotation abroad and travel, and pride in being an employee of the venture. This information should signal to JV managers that new and creative ways of rewarding and recognizing employees for performance are worthy of exploration.

A COMMITMENT TO CHANGE

Western investors in Central/Eastern Europe have an important and critical role in the development of economies in that region. The com-mitment of capital, technical, and managerial expertise as part of a long-range plan of investment has the potential to offer great benefits to local managers and employees. Local people see the formation of joint ventures in their communities as a sign of faith by the Western partner in the development of the area following the Socialist legacy. They view partici-pation by the West in countries such as Poland, Hungary, and the Czech Republic as a way to facilitate the transition to economic levels more com-patible with those enjoyed in the West. Local managers and employees are hungry for change, and, in general, people are working extremely hard to advance to new heights as members of the European community.

There is no doubt the West has a key and accountable role in the ev-olution of transition economies in Central/Eastern Europe. According to Bugajski (1991), "Eastern Europe has entered a critical period of political turbulence, economic restructuring, and social dislocation that could pre-cipitate domestic and international instability." Although Western busi-nesses are interested in the profitability of their investments, an influx of Western capital and technology into joint ventures in Eastern and Central Europe can potentially contribute to the long-term stability of the region. Related to broader requirements for national stability, Czinkota (1991: 26) writes,

This will require major programs designed to alter the determinants of national advantage of the Eastern European nations and involve funding, training, invest-ment, and technology sharing. Not doing so would result in a major failure of the

West and a major threat to the continued viability of the EC [European Community]. It must be understood that instability does not just result from tanks, but also from the knowledge that the next-door neighbor lives in poverty-driven volatility.

Through long-term commitment to joint venture activity, stability to the democratization process might feasibly be encouraged.

If joint venture success between East-West partners is to be measured by employee commitment and productivity, then the nurturing of an environment in which local and foreign employees can learn together is a fundamental consideration. Learning evolves not only from technical training, but more importantly from a process where foreign managers are able to share responsibility with local managers—and to discard a mentality that management practices in the West are best. Development of mutual trust and respect for culture is imperative. Ideally, both local and foreign partners will seek to learn more about one another, in a relationship where new values and norms unique to the requirements of the joint venture are created.

The real potential for learning in East-West joint ventures is subtle, and is related to a configuration of culture, strategy, and structure. Unidimensional views of how learning evolves in complex organizations is clearly not satisfactory. Openness, flexibility, relativity, and commitment remain the veritable keys to large-scale organizational change. In the Central/ Eastern European context change has been remarkable and quick, despite external and environmental constraints. Long-term commitment by the foreign partner is imperative—with an emphasis on learning through people.

LESSONS LEARNED

Rare opportunities for learning are missed in joint ventures between Eastern and Western partners when local managers are not involved in the change process. Mutual respect and an admission that the West does not know best are imperative. Managers must be willing to share responsibility with employees, who in turn agree to actively embrace change. Of special importance is the creation of a new corporate culture for the joint venture in which norms for a more market-oriented and competitive system are implemented in a context that has relevance for the local employees.

To summarize, learning and change in joint ventures in Central/Eastern Europe are facilitated when:

• expatriate managers have knowledge of the local culture and are sensitive to the concerns of local employees;

- strategy is focused on attaining results;
- goal setting and feedback are emphasized in order that a new direction for employees can be monitored;
- training is broad for all employees, with a special emphasis on new skill acquisition for mid-level managers; and
- rewards are performance-based and reinforce new ideologies.

NOTE

1. Information about the joint ventures described in this chapter was collected in Hungary, Poland, and the Czech Republic during the period from December 1992 to March 1993. Data and insights were obtained from extensive interviews with senior managers and other employees, coupled with survey questionnaires (1,200 returned).

CHAPTER 15

Toward the Future

> Human relations are going to be the key strategic issues in joint ventures. Those who understand this will be able to build healthy and long-lasting relationships, because of their focus on the "invisible assets" of every quality-oriented organisation: human beings—their knowledge, creativity, and commitment.
>
> Csath (1991: 89)

HRM in joint ventures is expected to look different from HRM in other forms of organizations. Joint ventures are especially complicated, and consequently HR managers must be attuned to the demands of managers and employees from different organizational contexts or different cultural backgrounds. An area of special importance is the management of the JV-parent relationship when at least three intact entities (i.e., the parents and joint venture) are interfaced. The assignment of the management contract to one parent is in many ways a political gesture and must be managed as such. Special challenges exist for HR managers to adapt the joint venture and its staff to rapidly changing competitive and strategic realities.

HR managers answer to numerous stakeholders, and face many opportunities as well as constraints. As an HR manager at Diamond Star mused, it is like "tap dancing on bonfires all the time." At times, the heat is intense. HR managers require a depth of understanding that goes beyond traditional requirements—an understanding that includes knowledge of the parent cultures, JV employee needs and insecurities, strategic initiatives, and how learning at the organizational level can be nurtured to meet ever-changing internal and external environmental demands.

GLOBAL ORGANIZATIONS OF THE PRESENT AND FUTURE

Joint ventures are not a new phenomena, nor are they "trendy." They are definitely on the increase. Joint ventures are one mechanism by which multinational companies can expand in a world where there are international trading blocks (i.e., Far East, Europe, and North America), and increased requirements to be "close to the customer" in locations in various countries. Parent firms join to share risks or technology, and to be better positioned to create and market innovative, high-quality, cost-efficient products.

In Central and Eastern Europe, JV activity has rapidly increased since the fall of Communism in 1989, with Hungary leading the way with volume of JV start-ups. At the end of 1989, 1,590 joint ventures operated in Hungary (11 percent of all companies); by the end of 1990, 5,000 joint ventures were in operation, representing 35 percent of all companies (Csath, 1991). The numbers continue to rise. Further, in the wake of the NAFTA agreement between the United States, Canada, and Mexico, JV activity along the Mexican border with the United States has continued to escalate as investors seek viable partnerships, and entry to new markets. The Pacific Rim is considered by many to be the economic bridge to the twenty-first century, and joint ventures are the primary vehicle for investment in that region.

Although joint ventures are often considered in relation to the advantages they offer for international competitiveness and financial returns, there may also be less tangible benefits from the formation of such partnerships. For instance, in international joint ventures between partners from diverse national cultures, opportunities for cultural learning and exchange may result. In addition, joint ventures can provide a vehicle by which capital and technical skills can be transferred into countries (e.g., in Central or Eastern Europe) where newly emerging democracies are struggling to stabilize. Long-term committed participation by the partners to the venture, rather than short-term and quick-gain involvements, will most likely result in JV successes. Benefits to the local economy and workforce can be provided during periods of social, economic, and political change.

AN EMPHASIS ON LEARNING IN JOINT VENTURE FIRMS

Throughout this book a broad and creative role for HRM has been outlined. The HRM function is operated at various levels, not only by HR managers and staff but also by a wide range of other employees in the venture and parent firms. In Chapter 6 a process role for HRM is outlined that transcends traditional roles or functions. HR managers can operate as facilitators, integrators, creators of norms and values, and cultural liaisons—if given the opportunity and if there is the desire to do so. More specifically, HRM activities in joint ventures are proposed to involve (1) management of the JV-parent relationship; (2) integration of HRM and strategy; (3) development of norms and values that support the strategic objectives of the JV and parent firms; (4) sensitivity to national culture issues and the creation of culturally appropriate HR policy; and (5) the facilitation of an environment where learning can flourish.

Given the wide and multifaceted role for HRM, one might expect that in the future even greater flexibility and a focus on learning in the organization will be key considerations for company competitiveness and survival. Watkins and Marsick (1993: 8-9) described organizational learning in the following way:

The learning organization is one that learns continuously and transforms itself. Learning takes place in individuals, teams, the organization, and even the communities with which the organization interacts. Learning is a continuous, strategically used process—integrated with, and running parallel to, work. Learning results in changes in knowledge, beliefs, and behaviors. Learning also enhances organizational capacity for innovation and growth. The learning organization has embedded systems to capture and share learning.

Learning requires managers to be open and willing to suspend their need for control. McGill, Slocum, and Lei (1991) suggest learning-oriented managers demonstrate cultural awareness and "humility" which respects the values and customs of others. They state, "cultural-functional narrowness and/or ethnocentricity results in an educated incapacity that reduces the ability of organizations and managers to learn" (p. 11). Learning is fostered by flexibility and a willingness to take risks.

With respect to the joint ventures described in this book, learning is considered to operate in three ways that fall within the mandate of HRM in joint venture firms. Learning occurs (1) related to the parent-parent or parent-JV goals and expectations for the venture, (2) in administrative areas including policy changes, and (3) related to technology sharing and technical innovations. Relevant issues pertaining to how learning evolves in joint ventures are elaborated in the following sections.

Partner Learning

Goals and expectations between the parents and between the parents and the joint venture are bound to change over time. This necessitates a process in which the partners build relationships and establish channels for communication in order that they may continue to learn about each other. In international ventures, willingness by the partners to learn about each other is an important component of collaboration. This includes both learning between the parents, and learning between the parents and the venture related to tasks, goals, and expectations.

In early JV negotiations, specific partner goals are usually determined. For example, one partner may be given the marketing responsibility for the venture, the other partner may supply raw resources. However, over time the original responsibilities or expectations of the partners may begin to shift. At Mayo Forest Products after ten years of partnership, the parents recognized a refocusing and separation of the parent roles was required. Both parent companies set out to redefine their involvement in the joint venture, and to determine each partner's expectations as part of the re-organization plan for the mill. Alternately, without ongoing attention to changed requirements, and a willingness to alter values and priorities as a consequence, the JV partners may eventually find that initial strategic goals are no longer in alignment.

In addition, the assignment of management responsibility to one part-ner sets a tone for how the joint venture will be managed. At Siecor some executives from the non-managing parent firm eventually felt they would like more direct HR involvement in the venture, considering their 50 percent equity stake. As a result, the HR manager at Siecor noted she ideally would establish mechanisms through which both parents can con-tribute to policy formation in the venture. Further, the effective manage-ment of the JV-parent relationship involves balancing stakeholder interests in order that power struggles don't erupt between parent groups to the detriment of the joint venture. JV managers need to manage the process wherein the joint venture has sufficient autonomy to develop systems unique to the venture and its needs, as opposed to simply adapting poli-cies or programs from the parent firms.

Doz and Schuen (1991: 14-15) suggest "the importance and necessity of developing, building and continuing learning about the partner's or-ganization, culture and ways is underestimated as compared to other types of more explicit and measurable learning." Further, insufficient learning among the partners may be a hidden cause for venture failure. Related to this possibility, greater attention might be focused on the parent-parent or parent-JV relationships. The development of norms for information exchange, joint communication networks, and specific mechanisms for conflict resolution when normal communication channels falter may all be important to continued JV success. In the joint ventures described here, collaboration was nurtured through the JV board structure and ad-visory committees, other formalized meetings, and informal contacts be-tween executives. The development of communication networks that span different international locations and JV groups helped to build intercul-tural and strategic understanding.

Administrative Learning

As technical demands change, and as parent involvement or control in the venture is modified, original JV management systems are likely to become obsolete. External demands that were largely market driven formed the impetus for change at Mayo Forest Products and Siecor. The parameters for management involvement at Mayo were revised as the parents redefined their roles and responsibilities in the venture. In each of the above cases, policy changes are likely to be required to match new conditions in the organization.

More specifically, HRM policy did change to keep pace with revised strategic demands. Further, at Mayo Forest Products, OCG, Siecor, and Diamond Star, HR managers selectively contributed to the creation of HR policy that supports organizational learning through:

- verbal feedback to employees for ideas or suggestions and an effort by managers to implement employee suggestions in practice (all four joint ventures);
- recognition programs for employee efforts and accomplishments (Mayo, OCG, Siecor); Diamond Star recognizes QC performance;
- financial awards (OCG and Siecor have cash bonuses for technological and commercial accomplishments);
- hiring well-educated personnel with broad-based abilities (all four joint ventures);
- training that focuses on broad skills with an emphasis on quality and innovation (all four joint ventures);
- transfers of employees between the parents and the joint venture for the exchange of management and technological expertise (Siecor, Diamond Star); and
- performance appraisal that considers innovative contributions (Siecor).

Also of relevance in JV firms is sensitivity to the specific needs of minority groups in the venture. At OCG, a special role for the HR group involved the successful integration of a minority group of parent employees into the joint venture. Similarly, at Diamond Star, the HR staff was involved in the implementation of "hybrid" HR policy that matched the needs of Japanese managers who were initially uncomfortable with a performance appraisal system. More generally, then, HR managers can operate as barometers in the organization, monitoring and creating effective policy initiatives in tune with the sensitivities of diverse subgroups in the venture.

Technological Learning

Although various HR strategies contribute to innovation and learning in joint ventures, at Mayo, OCG, Siecor, and Diamond Star staffing and training for the purpose of technological learning are of particular importance. In the area of staffing, transfers of personnel contribute to the introduction of necessary skills to the venture. Senior executives are transferred to the joint venture from the parents with the specific goal of bringing technical proficiencies with them. For example, at Siecor, the Vice-President of Cable Technology is from Siemens and was responsible for the introduction of essential cable expertise to the venture. In addition, large numbers of technical staff are transferred to the ventures in order to introduce new technical skills into the joint venture. At Diamond Star, Japanese technical assistants on temporary assignment from Mitsubishi train production workers in Japanese manufacturing methods. Further, counterbalanced staffing between Japanese and American executives at Diamond Star is another mechanism through which managers can exchange technical (and administrative or cultural) knowledge.

Training is likewise a priority in the joint ventures and generally is considered to contribute to the level of technological learning. At Diamond Star, JV staff received training in Japan, as well as from Japanese on assignment to the venture. In addition, cross-training occurs at Siecor and Diamond Star; job rotation operates at Diamond Star. Staff placements into cross-functional teams and task groups at OCG serve to create a broader technical learning base between the research and manufacturing arms of that operation.

HRM AS A FLUID PROCESS

HRM in joint ventures—perhaps in all forms of organizations—is better conceptualized as a process than as a discrete set of policies and programs. This process differs in each organization depending on the corporate strategy, products, locations, employees and their needs, and other relevant internal or external demands. HRM has fluid boundaries and is initiated at all levels of the company, from HR staff to managers and executives, to production employees who are given autonomy to design HR systems for themselves and their peers. In international joint ventures, the fluidity of boundaries extends beyond the simple organizational form itself to include interorganizational relationships between the parent firms and the venture.

Rather than operating in a single set of "context conditions," HRM is proposed to exist within a multi-dimensional framework. This frame has been outlined in various ways throughout this book and more specifically considers how HR activities (e.g., communication, staffing, training, reward and recognition, and performance appraisal) are construed in the context of the JV-parent interface, strategy, and culture. Within an ideal set of parameters, HRM is responsive to the unique conditions in the joint venture. For example, in joint ventures in Central/Eastern Europe the determination of new and flexible reward structures will be a primary consideration, as managers strive to create incentives for employees to excel beyond what was expected in the Communist system. In culturally diverse joint ventures (e.g., between Japanese and American partners), the development of HR policy and practice is expected to differ from that of culturally similar JV firms. A prerequisite to the development of fluid HR systems is the allocation of flexible people with broad skills in the joint venture. It is no coincidence that in the joint ventures described in this book, including the ventures in Central/Eastern Europe, staffing emphasizes personal rather than technical capabilities. People are the key to the development of effective and strategically-oriented HR or other systems. HRM is built on history—with a vision to the future. It is based on awareness, integrity, and openness to learning and change. Capturing optimism about a joint venture located in the Czech Republic, a German manager states,

With such a project, we demonstrate we are optimistic about the future. We trust in the people. We are convinced that we will be the best in Europe. . . . With this skill of the people, I believe I have no fear about accomplishing this objective. . . . Technology is not so important in comparison to the people.

Appendixes

APPENDIX 1

Description of HRM Activities

In the present context, HRM includes:

Communication—Systems for communication operate at multiple levels in the organization and may include, for example, meetings, written correspondence, television or telephone. Schein (1986) notes that communication may be either formal and insitutionalized, or informal. In addition, communication may be open and generally involve employees, or closed and specific to selected group members. As the complexity of the organization increases, forms of communication such as transition teams, task forces, or joint-management teams may be used to create information linkages across diverse and often geographically decentralized groups (Barlett and Ghoshal, 1989; Joiner, 1987; Kanter, 1983; Prahalad and Doz, 1987).

Staffing—Staffing is usually defined as searching for and obtaining potential job candidates in sufficient amount and quality in order that the organization can renew itself and fill job needs. Staffing objectives are also concerned with satisfying the needs of job candidates. Not only should job applicants be attracted to an organization, but it is desirable that they be retained. Staffing may be done internal or external to the organization, follow broad or narrow career paths, offer single or multiple promotional ladders, use explicit or implicit criteria for promotion, or use closed or open (i.e., job postings) procedures.

Reward/Recognition—Reward systems are the mechanism by which organizations seek to evaluate the contributions of employees in order that direct and indirect monetary and non-monetary rewards can be distributed. Rewards are provided based on legal regulations and the organization's ability to pay. Reward will vary according to whether there exists high or low base salaries; internal or external equity; few or many "perks"; and flexible or fixed and standardized packages. Rewards may encourage employee participation; have incentives built in; be based on short-term or long-term incentives; have employment security; and be either hierarchical or egalitarian-based.

Training—Training and development activities refer to an attempt to improve employee performance through new skill or knowledge acquisition, or the adjustment of employee attitudes. Training may focus on short-term or long-term needs, and narrow or broad applications (i.e., productivity versus quality of work life). Training may be planned and systematic or spontaneous, or may be unplanned or unsystematic; may have a group or individual orientation; and may allow low or high employee participation.

Performance Appraisal—As a formal structure, performance appraisal (PA) is a system which measures, evaluates, and influences an employee's attributes, behaviors, and performance. Data obtained from the appraisal may be used to correct employee deficiencies or to suggest alternative job placements for an employee. Appraisal may vary according to whether the process emphasizes how well an employee does a job versus how many things an employee accomplishes; whether criteria are behaviorally or results oriented; the extent to which evaluation criteria are short-term or long-term; whether the purpose is developmental, maintenance, or remedial; the degree of employee participation expected; and whether individual or group appraisal criteria are stressed.

APPENDIX 2

Methodology, Interview Questions, and Questionnaires

METHODOLOGY FOR THE INVESTIGATION

The Format

Data were collected between April and August 1991. I had a "contact person" in each joint venture, who assisted in the arrangement of interviews, suggested meetings to attend, outlined relevant documents to collect (and often provided them), and informed me about miscellaneous items of company protocol. The operations of the joint ventures were not usually contained in a single location. Subsequently, to gain a broader perspective of the operations, I visited more than one site to collect information or materials for this project.

The Interviews

The interview format was consistent for all participants. I would introduce myself and the research topic, ask participants if they had any questions, request permission to tape-record the session, and get the participation consent form signed. Confidentiality was discussed, and participants had two options: I could use names with statements they made, or confidentiality would be guaranteed. This portion of the consent form was completed at the end of the interview, in order that participants could better judge their preference based upon what they had already said. No one refused to have the session tape-recorded. To lead participants into the interviews gradually, we began with the participant describing his or her background and experience, and the work role in the venture. I did not take notes, but chose to have a "conversation" with the individual who was interviewed. The interviews were relatively unstructured and I used open-ended questions as probes. Participants were encouraged to include any information they felt was relevant to help me understand how and why HRM policy and practice operated as it did in the venture. On average, the interviews were one and one-half to two hours in length. Refer to the outline of interview questions included in Appendix 3.

The Minnesota Job Satisfaction Questionnaire

The short form of the Minnesota Job Satisfaction Questionnaire (MSQ) developed by Weiss, Dawis, England, and Lofquist (1967) was completed by a random sample of employees in each venture. The questionnaire has been used over the years as a reliable measure of job satisfaction (Muchinsky, 1983). The short version of the inventory consists of 20 items related to various aspects of one's job. The employee responds on a five-point scale. In addition to an overall score for job satisfaction (which is a summation of scores on all MSQ items), there are two subscales which determine employee levels of "intrinsic" and "extrinsic" job satisfaction. The intrinsic satisfaction scale consists of 12 items that reflect achievement, ability utilization, and autonomy, for example. The extrinsic scale consists of six items that relate to policy administration or working conditions. The MSQ manual indicates that internal consistency (based on a wide variety of occupational groups) has a mean reliability coefficient of .86 for the intrinsic satisfaction scale, .80 for the extrinsic scale, and .90 for the general satisfaction scale.

This research focuses on the organizational level of employee responses to job satisfaction, rather than on individual level responses. For this reason, mean scores and standard deviations for each item of the MSQ are aggregated across all respondents in a joint venture. Aggregated mean scores for overall job satisfaction, and category scores for intrinsic and extrinsic levels of job satisfaction, were obtained. As suggested in the test manual, it is most meaningful to consider scores for overall satisfaction, intrinsic satisfaction, and extrinsic satisfaction compared to percentile ratings. A high degree of job satisfaction is represented in the 75th percentile or higher, mid-range satisfaction is the 26th-74th percentile, and a low degree of job satisfaction is reflected in the 25th percentile or lower. A sample copy of the questionnaire appears in Appendix 3.

The Culture Inventory

The Culture Inventory considers various aspects of corporate culture as it operates within a company. The inventory has 12 items adopted from Quinn's (1984) competing values model. Four types of corporate culture are represented (three items for each culture type). The various culture orientations include group, developmental, hierarchical, and rational cultures. Participants respond on a five-point scale to indicate their level of agreement with each of the 12 statements in the inventory. I made one modification to the original inventory and changed "participant's business" to "this company" which I felt would be more relevant to the respondents in my sample. According to Yeung et al. (1989), who have also used this inventory in research with a large sample of companies, the reliability coefficients for the four culture types are: group culture (.79), developmental culture (.80), hierarchical culture (.76), and rational culture (.77). The level of cultural predominance in each of the four culture categories is determined by adding numerical responses for each group of three items. As with the MSQ, organizational level responses were obtained in each joint venture. Scores for the Culture Inventory are represented as aggregated means for each item of the inventory. Mean scores were also obtained for each of the four corporate culture categories. A copy of the questionnaire appears in Appendix 3.

GUIDELINE QUESTIONS ON HRM POLICY AND PRACTICE

Background Questions

- Explain the HRM role in this company.
- What are the unique issues HRM faces in alliance firms (i.e., cultural, political, technical)?
- How can HRM assist in dealing with these unique challenges?

INTRODUCTION

1. Overall, to what extent has HRM policy and practice changed over time? Describe. Why did these changes occur?
2. Which HRM policies operate most successfully? Why? Which policies are problematic? Why?

PLANNING

How are the needs of different groups of employees accommodated?

3. Are there HRM practices in place for accommodating diverse (cultural) needs of employees in the IJV? If so, have these practices changed over time? Is cultural sensitivity demonstrated in employee/management behaviors? Are the same HRM policies applied to all IJV employees? Explain.

Are there mechanisms for building trust between employees and managers? Explain.

4. Is information shared among IJV managers and employees? If information is shared, how much? content? When is miscommunication most likely?

5. Are there mechanisms for facilitating communication and collaboration between management and employees of the IJV? (i.e., task forces, steering committees, transition teams, information sharing sessions) If so, when are they formed? membership? Are there meetings? newsletters?

How are conflicts resolved when they arise?

6. Who in your group (or in the organization) is involved in problem-solving?

STAFFING

How are staffing decisions made (for managers and workers)?

7. How was the general manager chosen? the senior manager of HRM? other managers? (when?)

8. Are the same selection criteria used for all managers and employees? Describe.

9. Which qualities are valued in managers? workers (i.e., analytic ability, interpersonal skills, flexibility, cultural sensitivity, language skills)? Evidence?

10. Who makes staffing decisions (i.e., are employees or department heads involved)?

PERFORMANCE APPRAISAL

Describe the performance appraisal process.

11. What is the purpose of appraisals (i.e., developmental, remedial, maintenance)?

12. What actions are taken based on the appraisal?

13. Who provides the appraisals? Who is appraised?

14. What kind of rating criteria are used in appraisals (i.e., interpersonal skills, contribution to team effort, etc.)

15. How often are appraisals performed?

16. Is the same appraisal process applied to all managers and employees?

17. Are cultural factors taken into account?

TRAINING

How are training programs developed and implemented?

18. What is the focus of training (i.e., job content, problem-solving, cultural, communication skills)? What are the values communicated?

19. Who provides the training (parents, IJV)?

20. Who develops the training packages?

21. What is the format for training?

22. Is the aim to transfer "know how" from the parent to the IJV or the other way?

23. Are training programs culture-specific or multicultural? Are different courses offered for employees from different cultures?

24. To what extent is job retraining done?

PROMOTION AND REWARD

How are promotions awarded?

25. What is the basis for promotion (seniority, ability)? Why?

26. Are promotion criteria the same for all employees?

27. Is career path information available? Are bulletins featuring promotion/hiring information visible?

How do compensation systems operate?

28. What is the objective of rewards (i.e., to attract, motivate, or retain employees)?

29. To what extent are employees involved in creating their own compensation packages?

30. Are the same reward systems applied to all employees? Is there a perception of equality or inequality of rewards? Explain.

31. Are there incentives for learning new skills or behaviors?

OTHER

- What are the major challenges to IJV managers?
- Are experimentation and creativity encouraged in the IJV? How?
- Is there anything else that should be added in order for me to understand how HRM policy and practice operates?

MINNESOTA JOB SATISFACTION QUESTIONNAIRE

Indicate the degree of satisfaction you have with your job. Ask yourself how satisfied you are with its various aspects.

Use the following guide for your answers:

VDS	**D**	**N**	**S**	**VS**
Very Dissatisfied	**Dissatisfied**	**Can't Decide**	**Satisfied**	**Very Satisfied**

Circle one alternative for each question.

1. Being able to keep busy all the time...........VDS D N S VS

2. The chance to work alone on the job...........VDS D N S VS

3. The chance to do different things from
   time to time...................................VDS D N S VS

4. The chance to be somebody in the community.....VDS D N S VS

5. The way my boss handles his people............VDS D N S VS

6. The competence of my supervisor in
   making decisions...............................VDS D N S VS

7. Being able to do things that don't go
   against my conscience..........................VDS D N S VS

8. The way my job provides for steady
   employment.....................................VDS D N S VS

9. The chance to do things for other people.......VDS D N S VS

10. The chance to tell people what to do...........VDS D N S VS

11. The chance to do something that makes use
    of my ability.................................VDS D N S VS

12. The way company policies are put into
    practice......................................VDS D N S VS

13. My pay and the amount of work I do.............VDS D N S VS

14. The chances for advancement on this job........VDS D N S VS

15. The freedom to use my own judgement............VDS D N S VS

16. The chance to try my own methods of
    doing the job.................................VDS D N S VS

17. The working conditions.........................VDS D N S VS

18. The way my co-workers get along with
    each other....................................VDS D N S VS

19. The praise I get for doing a good job..........VDS D N S VS

20. The feeling of accomplishment I get from
    the job.......................................VDS D N S VS

QUINN'S CULTURE INVENTORY

The following statements describe types of values which may exist in your company. None of the descriptions is better than the others. They are just different. Please indicate the extent to which each statement applies to the company where you work.
Show your degree of agreement or disagreement by circling the appropriate number as on the following scale.

1	2	3	4	5

Low Agreement   Moderate Agreement   High Agreement

1. This company is a very <u>personal</u> place. It is like an extended family. People share a lot of themselves...........1 2 3 4 5

2. This company is a very <u>dynamic</u> and <u>entrepreneurial</u> place. People are willing to stick their necks out and take risks.
    ....1 2 3 4 5

3. This company is a very <u>formal</u> and <u>structured</u> place. People pay attention to procedures to get things done...........1 2 3 4 5

4. This company is a very <u>production oriented</u> place. People are concerned with getting the job done..................1 2 3 4 5

5. The glue that holds this company together is <u>loyalty and tradition</u>. Commitment runs high....................1 2 3 4 5

6. The glue that holds this company together is <u>commitment to innovation and development</u>. There is an emphasis on being first with products and services....................1 2 3 4 5

7. The glue that holds this company together is <u>formal rules and policies</u>. Following rules is important..............1 2 3 4 5

8. The glue that holds this company together is an emphasis on <u>tasks and goal accomplishment</u>. A production and achievement orientation is shared...............................1 2 3 4 5

9. This company emphasizes <u>human resources</u>. Morale is important.
    ....1 2 3 4 5

10. This company emphasizes <u>growth through developing new ideas</u>. Generating new products or services is important.....1 2 3 4 5

11. This company emphasizes <u>permanence and stability</u>. Efficiency is important...1 2 3 4 5

12. This company emphasizes <u>outcomes and achievement</u>.

    Accomplishing goals is important.....................1 2 3 4 5

Background Information

It is important to have some information on the background of those people who respond to the questionnaires. Again, all information is strictly confidential.

Age: _____ years

Sex: _____ Male _____ Female

Highest level of education _____

Job title _____

Number of years in this company _____

Years of residence in this country _____

Ethnic Origin (if born outside this country) _____

Number of nonvacation days absent from work this year ____

              (year = one year prior from today's date)

Results of the Two Employee Questionnaires

Results from the Minnesota Job Satisfaction
Questionnaire at Mayo Forest Products
As Aggregated Scores Across All Respondents

Item	Mean	SD
1. Able to keep busy	4.34	.48
2. Chance to work alone	4.25	.76
3. Chance to do different things	3.65	1.23
4. Chance to be somebody in the community	3.69	.59
5. Way my boss handles people	3.00	1.15
6. Competence of supervisor's decisions	3.28	1.22
7. Able to do things that don't go against my conscience	3.88	.87
8. Job provides steady employment	4.53	.32
9. Chance to do things for others	4.16	.57
10. Chance to tell people what to do	3.69	.82
11. Job makes use of my ability	3.69	1.20
12. Way company policy is put into practice	2.47	1.27
13. Pay related to the amount of work	3.41	1.21
14. Chance for advancement	3.44	1.01
15. Freedom to use my judgement	3.93	1.07
16. Able to try my own methods	3.81	1.06
17. The working conditions	3.97	.86
18. The way coworkers get along	2.66	1.23
19. Praise for doing a good job	3.12	1.31
20. Feeling of accomplishment from the job	4.09	.82

Aggregated Category Scores

	Mean	SD	Percentile
Intrinsic Job Satisfaction (items 1-4, 7-11, 15, 16, 20)	47.65	6.05	79.42
Extrinsic Job Satisfaction (items 5, 6, 12, 13, 14, 19)	18.69	3.91	62.30
Total Job Satisfaction (items 1-20)	73.06	9.30	73.06

Results from the Culture Inventory
at Mayo Forest Products
As Aggregated Scores Across All Respondents

Item	Mean	SD
1. A personal place	2.09	1.30
2. Dynamic and entrepreneurial	2.59	1.21
3. Formal and structured	2.53	1.24
4. Production-oriented	3.84	.92
5. Loyalty and tradition	2.41	1.39
6. Commitment to innovation and development	3.81	1.06
7. Formal rules and policies	2.59	1.10
8. Tasks and goal accomplishment	3.13	1.31
9. Emphasis on human resources	2.43	1.39
10. Growth through new ideas	3.75	1.32
11. Permanence and stability	3.47	1.32
12. Outcomes and achievement	3.81	1.31

Aggregated Means for the Culture Categories

Group Culture	6.93
Developmental Culture	10.15
Hierarchical Culture	8.59
Rational Culture	10.78
Total Score	36.45

Results from the Minnesota Job Satisfaction
Questionnaire at OCG
As Aggregated Scores Across All Respondents

Item	Mean	SD
1. Able to keep busy	4.27	.80
2. Chance to work alone	4.21	.70
3. Chance to do different things	3.93	1.06
4. Chance to be somebody in the community	3.45	1.03
5. Way my boss handles people	3.18	1.16
6. Competence of supervisor's decisions	3.64	1.32
7. Able to do things that don't go against my conscience	4.03	.88
8. Job provides steady employment	4.03	1.13
9. Chance to do things for others	4.00	.88
10. Chance to tell people what to do	3.33	.96
11. Job makes use of my ability	3.57	1.39
12. Way company policy is put into practice	2.57	1.09
13. Pay related to the amount of work	2.94	1.27
14. Chance for advancement	2.81	1.31
15. Freedom to use my judgement	3.72	1.21
16. Able to try my own methods	3.81	1.10
17. The working conditions	3.48	1.06
18. The way coworkers get along	3.00	1.30
19. Praise for doing a good job	2.93	1.17
20. Feeling of accomplishment from the job	3.76	1.00

Aggregated Category Scores

	Mean	SD	Percentile
Intrinsic Job Satisfaction (items 1-4, 7-11, 15, 16, 20)	46.12	6.94	76.87
Extrinsic Job Satisfaction (items 5, 6, 12, 13, 14, 19)	18.09	5.61	60.30
Total Job Satisfaction (items 1-20)	70.69	13.14	70.69

Results from the Culture Inventory
at OCG
As Aggregated Scores Across All Respondents

	Item	Mean	SD
1.	A personal place	2.27	1.10
2.	Dynamic and entrepreneurial	2.18	1.04
3.	Formal and structured	2.73	1.15
4.	Production-oriented	3.48	1.09
5.	Loyalty and tradition	2.39	1.14
6.	Commitment to innovation and development	3.48	1.12
7.	Formal rules and policies	2.85	1.37
8.	Tasks and goal accomplishment	3.09	1.21
9.	Emphasis on human resources	2.48	1.25
10.	Growth through new ideas	3.45	1.15
11.	Permanence and stability	2.91	1.44
12.	Outcomes and achievement	3.42	1.12

Aggregated Means for the Culture Categories

Group Culture	7.14
Developmental Culture	9.11
Hierarchical Culture	8.49
Rational Culture	9.99
Total Score	34.73

Results from the Minnesota Job Satisfaction
Questionnaire at Siecor
As Aggregated Scores Across All Respondents

Item	Mean	SD
1. Able to keep busy	4.38	.65
2. Chance to work alone	4.42	.62
3. Chance to do different things	4.24	.77
4. Chance to be somebody in the community	3.73	.69
5. Way my boss handles people	3.57	1.23
6. Competence of supervisor's decisions	3.82	1.11
7. Able to do things that don't go against my conscience	4.29	.66
8. Job provides steady employment	4.53	.62
9. Chance to do things for others	4.20	.66
10. Chance to tell people what to do	3.56	.97
11. Job makes use of my ability	3.89	1.05
12. Way company policy is put into practice	2.80	1.32
13. Pay related to the amount of work	3.29	1.27
14. Chance for advancement	2.98	1.34
15. Freedom to use my judgement	4.04	.93
16. Able to try my own methods	3.69	1.12
17. The working conditions	4.07	.81
18. The way coworkers get along	3.71	1.06
19. Praise for doing a good job	3.31	1.02
20. Feeling of accomplishment from the job	4.07	.89

Aggregated Category Scores

	Mean	SD	Percentile
Intrinsic Job Satisfaction (items 1-4, 7-11, 15, 16, 20)	49.02	6.20	81.70
Extrinsic Job Satisfaction (items 5, 6, 12, 13, 14, 19)	19.77	5.26	65.90
Total Job Satisfaction (items 1-20)	76.53	11.57	76.53

Results from the Culture Inventory
at Siecor
As Aggregated Scores Across All Respondents

	Item	Mean	SD
1.	A personal place	2.93	1.16
2.	Dynamic and entrepreneurial	2.44	1.08
3.	Formal and structured	3.00	1.28
4.	Production-oriented	3.60	1.14
5.	Loyalty and tradition	2.82	1.19
6.	Commitment to innovation and development	3.80	1.18
7.	Formal rules and policies	2.86	1.31
8.	Tasks and goal accomplishment	3.31	1.22
9.	Emphasis on human resources	2.73	1.39
10.	Growth through new ideas	3.84	1.04
11.	Permanence and stability	3.38	1.15
12.	Outcomes and achievement	3.73	1.01

Aggregated Means for the Culture Categories

Group Culture	8.48
Developmental Culture	10.08
Hierarchical Culture	9.24
Rational Culture	10.64
Total Score	38.44

Results from the Minnesota Job Satisfaction
Questionnaire at Diamond Star
As Aggregated Scores Across All Respondents

	Item	Mean	SD
1.	Able to keep busy	4.21	.74
2.	Chance to work alone	3.87	1.09
3.	Chance to do different things	3.68	1.34
4.	Chance to be somebody in the community	3.45	.95
5.	Way my boss handles people	2.68	1.44
6.	Competence of supervisor's decisions	2.92	1.30
7.	Able to do things that don't go against my conscience	3.89	.80
8.	Job provides steady employment	4.61	.55
9.	Chance to do things for others	3.58	.95
10.	Chance to tell people what to do	3.32	.74
11.	Job makes use of my ability	3.34	1.44
12.	Way company policy is put into practice	2.47	1.16
13.	Pay related to the amount of work	4.18	.95
14.	Chance for advancement	2.82	1.23
15.	Freedom to use my judgement	3.47	1.13
16.	Able to try my own methods	3.71	1.06
17.	The working conditions	3.81	1.06
18.	The way coworkers get along	3.24	1.10
19.	Praise for doing a good job	2.74	1.13
20.	Feeling of accomplishment from the job	3.47	1.06

Aggregated Category Scores

	Mean	SD	Percentile
Intrinsic Job Satisfaction (items 1-4, 7-11, 15, 16, 20)	44.60	8.42	74.33
Extrinsic Job Satisfaction (items 5, 6, 12, 13, 14, 19)	17.81	5.04	59.37
Total Job Satisfaction (items 1-20)	69.47	13.34	74.33

Results from the Culture Inventory
at Diamond Star
As Aggregated Scores Across All Respondents

	Item	Mean	SD
1.	A personal place	2.34	.97
2.	Dynamic and entrepreneurial	2.00	.93
3.	Formal and structured	2.50	1.06
4.	Production-oriented	3.50	1.11
5.	Loyalty and tradition	2.24	.97
6.	Commitment to innovation and development	2.92	1.15
7.	Formal rules and policies	3.03	1.17
8.	Tasks and goal accomplishment	3.00	.90
9.	Emphasis on human resources	2.53	1.25
10.	Growth through new ideas	3.11	1.11
11.	Permanence and stability	3.63	1.08
12.	Outcomes and achievement	3.47	1.06

Aggregated Means for the Culture Categories

Group Culture	7.11
Developmental Culture	8.03
Hierarchical Culture	9.16
Rational Culture	9.97
Total Score	34.27

References

Badaracco, J.L. and Ellsworth, R.R. (1989). *Leadership and the Quest for Integrity*. Boston: Harvard Business School Press.

Baird, L.S., Lyles, M.A., and Wharton, R. (1989). Attitudinal Differences Between American and Chinese Managers Regarding Joint Venture Management. Paper presented at the Academy of Management Meetings, Washington, D.C.

Barnett, C.K. (1990). The Michigan Global Agenda: Research and Teaching in the 1990s. *Human Resource Management, 29*, 1, 5–26.

Bartlett, C.A. and Ghoshal, S. (1989). *Managing Across Borders: The Transnational Solution*. Boston: Harvard Business School Press.

Bugajski, J. (1991). Eastern Europe in the Post-Communist Era. *Columbia Journal of World Business, 26*, 1, 5–9.

Cascio, W.F. and Serapio, M.G. (1991). Human Resources Systems in an International Alliance: The Undoing of a Done Deal? *Organizational Dynamics*, Winter, 63–74.

Collins, T.M. and Doorley, T.L. (1991). *Teaming up for the 90s: A Guide to International Joint Ventures and Strategic Alliances*. Homewood, IL: Business One Irwin.

Csath, M. (1991). Strategic Alliances: Joint Venturing in Central and Eastern Europe (Problems and Opportunities): The Case of Hungary. *International Review of Strategic Management, 2*, 2, 73–107.

Cyr, Dianne J. (1994). OCG Microelectronic Materials. In J. Roos (ed.), *European Casebook on Cooperative Strategies*, New York: Prentice-Hall.

Czinkota, M. (1991). The EC '92 and Eastern Europe: Effects of Integration vs. Disintegration. *Columbia Journal of World Business, 26*, 1, 20–27

Datta, D.K. and Rasheed, A.M.A. (1989). HRM Considerations in the Planning of Joint Ventures. In the *International Conference on Personnel/Human Resource Management Proceedings*, Hong Kong, 351–360.

Doz, Y. and Shuen, A. (1991). From Intent to Outcome: A Process Framework for Partnerships. Working paper, INSEAD.

Dymsza, W.A. (1988). Successes and Failures of Joint Ventures in Developing Countries: Lessons from Experience. In F. Contractor and P. Lorange (eds.), *Cooperative Strategies in International Business.* Toronto: Lexington Books, 403–424.

Evans, P.A. (1986). The Strategic Outcomes of Human Resource Management. *Human Resource Management, 25,* 1, 149–167.

Forward, G.E., Beach, D.E., Gray, D.A., and Quick, J.C. (1991). Mentofacturing: A Vision for American Industrial Excellence. *The Executive,* 5, 3, 32–44.

Frayne, C.A. and Geringer, J.M. (1989). The Strategic Use of Human Resource Management Techniques as Control Mechanisms in International Joint Ventures. In the *International Conference on Personnel/Human Resource Management Proceedings,* Hong Kong, 341–350.

Frost, P.J., Moore, L.F., Louis, M.R., Lundberg, C.C., and Martin, J. (1985). *Organizational Culture.* Beverly Hills, CA: Sage Publications.

Harrigan, K.R. (1985). *Strategies for Joint Ventures.* Toronto: Lexington Books.

Hergert, M. and Morris, D. (1988). Trends in International Collaborative Agreements. In F. Contractor and P. Lorange (eds.), *Cooperative Strategies in International Business.* Toronto: Lexington Books, 99–109.

Ishida, H. (1986). Transferability of Japanese Human Resource Management Abroad. *Human Resource Management, 25,* 1, 103–120.

Jaeger, A.M. (1986). Organization Development and National Culture: Where's the Fit? *Academy of Management Review, 11,* 1, 178–190.

Joiner, C.W., Jr. (1987). *Leadership for Change.* Cambridge, MA: Ballinger Publishing.

Kanter, R.M. (1983). *The Change Masters.* New York: Simon and Schuster.

Kanter, R.M. (1989). *When Giants Learn to Dance: Mastering the Challenges of Strategy, Management, and Career in the 1990s.* New York: Simon and Schuster.

Killing, J.P. (1983). *Strategies for Joint Venture Success.* New York: Praeger.

Killmann, R.H., Covin, T.J., and Associates. (1988). *Corporate Transformation: Revitalizing Organizations for a Competitive World.* San Francisco: Jossey-Bass.

Kouzes, J.M. and Posner, B.Z. (1987). *The Leadership Challenge: How to Get Extraordinary Things Done in Organizations.* San Francisco: Jossey-Bass.

Laurent, A. (1986). The Cross-cultural Puzzle of International Human Resource Management. *Human Resource Management, 25,* 1, 91–102.

Lei, D. and Slocum, J.W. (1991). Global Strategic Alliances: Payoffs and Pitfalls. *Organizational Dynamics,* Winter, 44–62.

Lewis, J.D. (1990). *Partnerships for Profit: Structuring and Managing Strategic Alliances.* New York: The Free Press.

Likert, R. (1967). *The Human Organization.* New York: McGraw-Hill.

Lorange, P. and Roos, J. (1992). *Strategic Alliances: Formation, Implementation and Evolution.* Oxford: Blackwell Business.

Lorange, P. and Roos, J. (1991). Why Some Strategic Alliances Succeed and Others Fail. *Journal of Business Strategy,* January/February, 25–30.

McGill, M.E., Slocum, J.W., and Lei, D. (1991). Management Practices in Learning Organizations. *Organizational Dynamics,* Summer, 5–17.

Mendenhall, M. and Black, S. (1990). A Contextual Approach to Understanding

Conflict Management in U.S./Japanese Joint Ventures. Paper presented at the International Western Academy of Management Meetings, Shizuoka, Japan.

Morgan, G. (1988). *Riding the Waves of Change: Developing Managerial Competencies for a Turbulent World.* San Francisco: Jossey-Bass.

Muchinsky, P.M. (1983). *Psychology Applied to Work: An Introduction to Industrial and Organizational Psychology.* Homewood, IL: Dorsey Press.

Ohmae, K. (1990). *The Borderless World: Power and Strategy in the Interlinked Economy.* New York: Harper Business.

Parkhe, A. (1991). Interfirm Diversity, Organizational Learning, Longevity in Global Strategic Alliances. *Journal of International Business Studies, 22,* 4, 579–601.

Peterson, R.B. and Shimada, J.Y. (1978). Sources of Management Problems in Japanese-American Joint Ventures. *Academy of Management Review, 3,* 796–804.

Phillips, S. (1989). When U.S. Joint Ventures with Japan Go Sour. *Business Week,* July, 30–31.

Pieper, R. (ed.) (1990). *Human Resource Management: An International Comparison.* Berlin: de Gruyter.

Prahalad, C.K. and Doz, Y.L. (1987). *The Multinational Mission: Balancing Local Demands and Global Vision.* New York.: The Free Press.

Pucik, V. (1988). Strategic Alliances with the Japanese: Implications for Human Resource Management. In F. Contractor and P. Lorange (eds.), *Cooperative Strategies in International Business.* Toronto: Lexington, 487–498.

Quinn, R.E. (1984). Applying the Competing Values Approach to Leadership: Toward an Integrative Framework. In J.G. Hunt, D.M. Hosking, C.A. Schriesheim, and R. Stewart (eds.), *Leaders and Managers: International Perspectives on Managerial Behavior and Leadership.* New York: Pergamon Press.

Schein, E. (1986). Are You Corporate Cultured? *Personnel Journal,* November, 83–96.

Schein, E. (1984). Coming to a New Awareness of Organizational Culture. *Sloan Management Review,* Winter, 3–16.

Schuler, R.S. (1989). Scanning the Environment: Planning for Human Resource Management and Organizational Change. *Human Resource Planning, 12,* 257–276.

Shenkar, O. and Zeira, Y. (1987). Human Resources Management in International Joint Ventures: Directions for Research. *Academy of Management Review, 12,* 3, 546–557.

Teagarden, M.B. and Von Glinow, M.A. (1989). Human Resource Management Factors in International Joint Venture Effectiveness: The Case of the PRC. *International Conference on Personnel/Human Resource Management Proceedings.* Hong Kong, 361–370.

Tichy, N.M. (1988). Setting the Global Human Resource Management Agenda for the 1990s. *Human Resource Management, 27,* 1, 1–18.

Tsui, A.S. (1987). Defining the Activities and Effectiveness of the Human Resource Department: A Multiple Constituency Approach. *Human Resource Management, 26,* 35–69.

Tyebjee, T. (1991). Strategic Alliances with the Japanese. Working paper, Santa Clara University.

Walton, R.E. and Lawrence, P.R. (eds.) (1985). *HRM Trends and Challenges.* Boston: Harvard Business School Press.

Watkins, K. and Marsick, V.J. (1993). *Sculpting the Learning Organization: Lessons in the Art and Science of Systemic Change.* San Francisco: Jossey-Bass.

Weiss, D.J., Dawis, R.V., England, G.W., and Lofquist, L.H. (1967). *Manual for the Minnesota Satisfaction Questionnaire. Minnesota Studies in Vocational Rehabilitation,* no. XXII. Minneapolis: Industrial Relations Center, University of Minnesota.

Yeung, A., Brockbank, W., and Ulrich, D. (1989). Organizational Culture and Human Resource Practices: An Empirical Assessment. Paper presented at the Academy of Management Meetings, Washington, D.C.

Index

About the Author

DIANNE J. CYR is an Adjunct Professor at Simon Fraser University in Vancouver, Canada, where she teaches international HRM and organization theory. She has conducted research in progressive international joint ventures in North America, as well as initiated a major investigation into HRM in joint ventures in Poland, Hungary, and the Czech Republic. She is the President of Global Alliance Management, which specializes in topics related to international joint ventures and strategic alliances, and has numerous publications on international human resource management.